THE BOOK OF
LODDISWELL

HEART OF THE SOUTH HAMS
A PHOTOGRAPHIC HISTORY OF THE PARISH

THE LODDISWELL PARISH HISTORY GROUP

HALSGROVE

First published in Great Britain in 1999

Copyright © 1999 The Loddiswell Parish History Group

British Library Cataloguing-in-Publication Data
A CIP record for this title is available from the British Library

ISBN 1 84114 030 9

HALSGROVE
PUBLISHING, MEDIA AND DISTRIBUTION

Halsgrove House
Lower Moor Way
Tiverton, Devon EX16 6SS
Tel: 01884 243242
Fax: 01884 243325
website: http://www.halsgrove.com

Printed and bound in Great Britain by Bookcraft Ltd., Midsomer Norton

CONTENTS

FOREWORD

Some 2000 years of the Christian tradition have shaped the world in which we live providing the basis for our legal system and so much of our art and literature. Christianity has been a powerful force for change everywhere, shaping the communities in which we live.

Much of the life of the village still centres on the time-honoured village institutions; the Church, the village shop, the pub, the Chapel and the Village Hall. Yet every village is unique in its way. None more so than Loddiswell in the south west of Devon. The book charts the changes of fortune of this remarkable village and bears witness to some of the characters and the sense of community which has bound it together for over 1000 years and will, I am convinced, hold it together for another millennium.

Rev. Roderick Withnell, 1999

The Loddiswell Parish History Group.
Left to right: Alan Saville, Irene Hulse, Karen Elliott, Sue Sweeney,
Russell Baker and Reg and Betty Sampson (in front).
(Absent: Hazel Lethbridge.)

ACKNOWLEDGEMENTS

The Book of Loddiswell could not have been written without the support of our small committee of Russell Baker, Karen Elliott, Irene Hulse, Hazel Lethbridge, Alan Saville and Sue Sweeney. Special thanks are given to Owen and Sheila Elliott and Walter Kernick for their vast knowledge of the parish through the years and their invaluable help in identifying people in the older photographs. To Muriel Carpenter for her contribution on the recent history of the Congregational Church. The notes on local history by the late Christian Michell and Margaret Common have proved to be an invaluable help in compiling the book. Specials thanks also to Audrey Walke for correcting the prose and proof reading. To Mike Glanville for his line drawings (reproduced on pages 66 and 173).

We would like to thank those who have lent photographs and provided interesting information: Nelly Baker, Jean Baker, Gordon and Janet Beckley, Beryl Brooking, Cyril Brooking, Rodney Brooking, Steve Bradley, Les Bimacombe, John Came, Ann Carpenter, Peter Carpenter, Frank Carpenter, Jim and Susan Carr, Mac Carter, Muriel Clarke, Cheryl Chadwick, John and Alison Common, Jim Coombes, Steve and Sally Dutton, Laskey Elliott, Hilary Field, Pete George, Hilda Harvey, Paul and Joy Harvey, Colin and Joyce Herbert, Walter and Eveline Hine, Suzanne Hine, Carol Hodder, Jennifer and John Hosking, Hilary Hudson, Ruth and Ken Hyne, Winnie Jeffery, Harold Joint, Ann Kelly, Albert Kendall, Ivor and Joan King, Harold Lethbridge, John Marsh, Rene Marshall, Diana Murry, Christine Morcombe, Bob Northcott, Heather Northmore, Percy Nunn, Sir William and Lady Peek, Bill Penwill, Donald Pethybridge, Audrey Pope, Suzanne Prout, Helen Robins, Jane Rose, Gwen Seldon and the late Bill Seldon, Dennis Sharland, Peter Sweet, Wally Tarr, Rachael Tate, Basil Taylor, Julian Tregelles, Delia Wallis, Sylvia and Les Walke, Gordon Waterhouse, Ted Westlake, Michael Winterton, Percy Withers, Alison Withnell, Jean Wood, Margaret Wootton, Eunice Yabsley. Also: The Cookworthy Museum, Kelly's and White's Directories (Trades in Loddiswell), the staff of Loddiswell Primary School, Loddiswell W.I. and President Sue Ryder, the Over Sixties Club and Chairman Roy Cole, the Short Mat Bowls Club and Chairman Fred King, the Football Club and past President Bill Reader.

Reg and Betty Sampson
Lilwell, 1999

View of Loddiswell Bridge and New Mill Bridge looking towards Loddiswell, 1900.

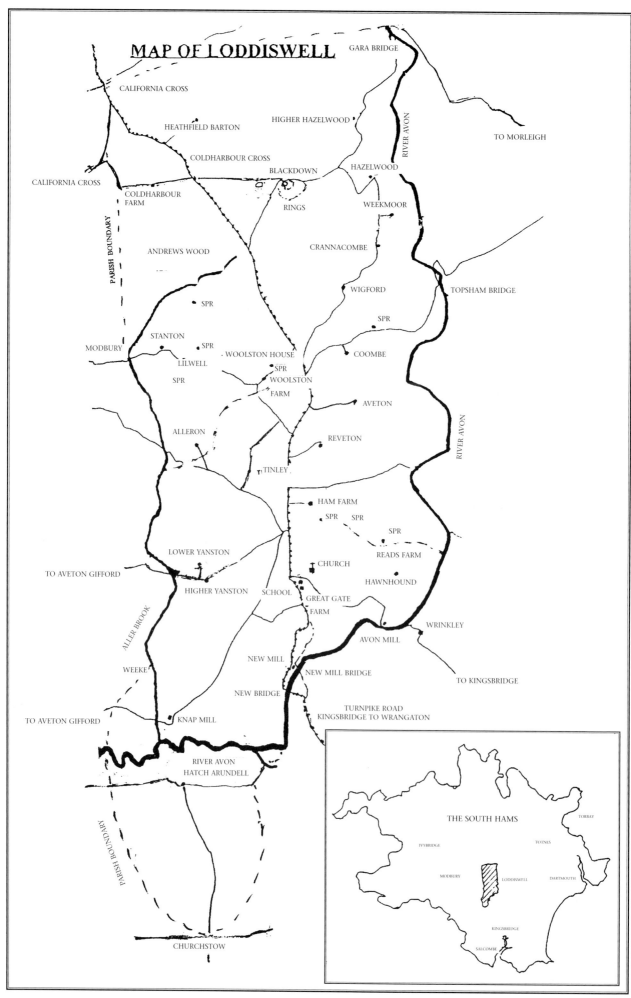

MAP OF LODDISWELL

GARA BRIDGE

CALIFORNIA CROSS

HEATHFIELD BARTON

HIGHER HAZELWOOD

RIVER AVON

TO MORLEIGH

COLDHARBOUR CROSS

BLACKDOWN

HAZELWOOD

CALIFORNIA CROSS

COLDHARBOUR FARM

RINGS

WEEKMOOR

PARISH BOUNDARY

ANDREWS WOOD

CRANNACOMBE

WIGFORD

TOPSHAM BRIDGE

SPR

SPR

STANTON

MODBURY

SPR

WOOLSTON HOUSE

COOMBE

LILWELL

SPR

SPR

WOOLSTON FARM

RIVER AVON

AVETON

ALLERON

REVETON

TINLEY

HAM FARM

SPR

SPR

LOWER YANSTON

SPR

READS FARM

TO AVETON GIFFORD

CHURCH

HAWNHOUND

HIGHER YANSTON

SCHOOL

GREAT GATE FARM

WRINKLEY

ALLER BROOK

AVON MILL

NEW MILL

NEW MILL BRIDGE

TO KINGSBRIDGE

WEEKE

NEW BRIDGE

TO AVETON GIFFORD

KNAP MILL

TURNPIKE ROAD
KINGSBRIDGE TO WRANGATON

RIVER AVON
HATCH ARUNDELL

PARISH BOUNDARY

THE SOUTH HAMS

TORBAY

IVYBRIDGE

TOTNES

MODBURY

LODDISWELL

DARTMOUTH

KINGSBRIDGE

CHURCHSTOW

SALCOMBE

Chapter 1: The Bones of Shire and Parish

Whether our names have appeared in local records for generations, or whether we have recently moved into the area for retirement and contentment; whether we look around us with comprehension or with indifference, we cannot alter the fact that the present has grown out of the past – that what we enjoy is an inheritance.

This is not a history book, for that book is inscribed in the shape of our fields and the names of our roads, woods, farms and villages. Each quirk of our boundary, every kink in a lane, is explained in it. But what we may not realize is that the intangibles – the laws we respect, the decencies and customs which we so often take for granted – they too are the experienced wisdom of our English predecessors who from Saxon times shaped our parish, named and largely built our church, and established forms of local government based upon agreement and the acceptance of Christian values.

It is a broad statement, but mainly true, that we in Loddiswell are still citizens of King Alfred's Kingdom of Wessex. Many peoples have settled or passed through the parish – Iron-Age men, Celts and even earlier races, who have left reminders – names like Avon, meaning 'a river', boundary dykes, and, of course, their genes, which are still with us.

Romans occupied our land for a long time, not penetrating much further westwards than Exeter, but when their legions were withdrawn to defend Rome, they left a vacuum which drew in tribes, raiders and settlers from Northern Europe, especially the Anglo-Saxons who came looking not for conquest or plunder, but for good land to farm. Substantial migrations of Romano-Celts to Brittany had left these parts nearly empty and there was plenty of room for all, so those left behind were tolerated and absorbed – a very English characteristic. It was the Saxons who cleared wildwood for farmland, drained swampy rivers into their present beds, introduced flocks and herds, and established homesteads and communications between markets. The Christian Church was central, the parish system and the hundreds set up, and Loddiswell took on the shape still recognized today.

Often and fiercely they had to fight pagan Danes and Vikings, and were perhaps slow to realise that an island can only be defended at sea. The ruthless, efficient Normans looked across the waters with envy, to a prosperous, well-governed, rich kingdom, and they accomplished what has been called the most successful conquest in Euro-

The stunning, undulating countryside of the Avon Valley looking towards Churchstow.

pean history, simply throwing Saxon landowners out and imposing their own people. They contributed little; only their names, which they added to the already settled manors and markets they had seized. Hence Berry Pomeroy, Hatch Arundell, Newton Ferrers, Bishopsteignton, etc. But we speak the English language, not Norman-French; our common law is home-made; our villages and landmarks have English names; our customs and attitudes are our own priceless inheritance, not alien impositions, and they could not change the English character, nor the green hills and vales that nourished it.

Lovingly improved by Elizabeth's yeomen, enriched and beautified by Georgian landlords, the land continues to evolve under the direction of today's farmers, with changing crops and with machines taking on the work of horses and oxen, yet the countryside embracing us is still recognizably theirs. So when next we hear a band of ringers pealing our bells across the parish, we may reflect upon our good fortune with enlarged gratitude!

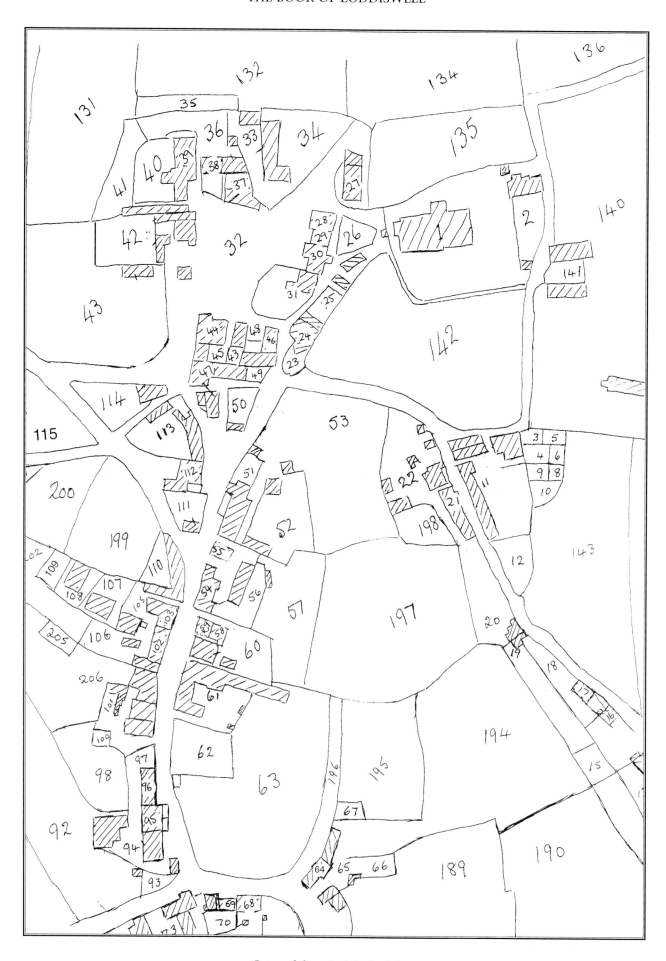

Copy of the 1839 Tithe Map.

1839 TITHE MAP. DESCRIPTION OF PROPERTIES. LODDISWELL

1	CHURCH of St Michael & All Angels
2	POOR HOUSES
3-10	Well Street (Bassetts) north side near Joey's Lane
11-12	" " Terrace east side of the road
13-20	Station Road. Terrace and various houses on west side of road
21	Well Street. Terrace on west side
22	Pond
23	Stables
24	Cottages (Hillside)
25	BLACKSMITH'S SHOP of John Kennard (Storridge)
26	Feoffees' garden let to Elizabeth Taylor
27	House and garden of Robert Popplestone (Corner House)
28	Elizabeth Taylor's house let to Robert Tucker
29	Barn used by Thomas Saunders
30	Feoffees' CHURCH HOUSE INN let to Elizabeth Taylor
31	Armanell Luscombe's house and garden
32	Courtledge
33-35	Court House and garden of James Friend
36	John Gillard's house and garden let to Nicholas Gillard (Tyepitte Cottage)
37	" " " " " " " " " (Tyepitte House)
38	Andrew Moreshead's house and garden let to Thomas Williams (Tyepitte Cottage)
39	Feoffees' JAIL HOUSE and another cottage let to James Crabbe and Robert Popplestone
40	Houses and gardens let to Mary Hine and John Hine (Peartree Cottage)
41	Let to John Tallman and William Terry (Hyne's Garage)
42	Feoffees' house and gardens let to James Friend
43	Feoffees' PARISH STABLE and orchard (Allotments, then car park and telephone exchange)
44	House, SHOP and cottages (Post Office and Whitelocks)
45	THE VILLAGE POUND
46	House and garden (Myrtle Cottage)
47-49	Various houses (Virginia, Bay Tree, Prospect and East Cottages)
50	Linhay and garden
51-53	House, gardens and orchard of Thomas Saunders and others (Wyselands)
54	House of George Rundle and Edward Bond (Phoenix Place)
55	POUND HOUSE let to John Prowse (London House Stores)
56	House and gardens (Pitt Court)
57	Orchard let to John Foxworthy
58	House of Nicholas Wills
59	House of James Friend of Toope's Tenement.
60	House and garden of Richard Jarvis
61	John King's homestead
62	Garden (Congregational Chapel)
63	Orchard (Loddiswell British School - now Primary School)
64	BLACKSMITH'S SHOP of Richard Jarvis
65	Feoffees of Slapton's Little Gate Tenement
66	House and garden of Richard Jarvis
67	Feoffees of Slapton's garden let to William Denbow
68	Thomas and John Rundle's Hillside House

69	Scoble Cottage
70-71	House, garden and orchard let to Henry Yollond (The Old Manse)
72-73	James King's homestead and garden (Cross House)
74-75	Tucker's Tenement. Homestead of John Treeby (Greystones)
76	Garden of Nicholas Prettijohn.
77	Richard Willing's MALT HOUSE and orchard (Vine Terrace)
78	John Treeby's house and garden let to John Hill ('Groots' or Vine House)
79-80	Orchards
81	Nicholas Prettijohn's courtlage and yard
82-83	John Denbow's house, court and gardens
84	Nicholas Prettijohn's garden
85-88	Richard Willing's homestead, orchards and garden (Mead Court)
89-90	Richard Crocker's garden let to Samuel Wakeham and William Moore
91	John King's Long Mead orchard
92-94	Public House, garden and orchard let to Thomas Rundle (New Bridge Inn)
95-97	Houses, courtlage and gardens let to Richard Lidstone, Robert Tucker and Samuel Brown
98	Peggy and Frances White's house and garden
99	House and garden let to George Luscombe
100-1	House, yard and garden let to Samuel Brown
102-6	Houses and gardens
107	Houses and gardens let to Joseph Gay, Robert Codd and Isaac Popplestone
108	FIRST CONGREGATIONAL CHAPEL
109	Garden (Chapel Yard)
110	John Guest's house, cottages and SCHOOL ROOM (Elliott's Shop and cottages)
111	Thomas Saunder's BLACKSMITH'S SHOP
112	Thomas Rundle's TURK'S HEAD INN (Loddiswell Inn)
113	House and garden of Thomas Willing, BUTCHER
114	Thomas Saunders orchard, cow house and garden (Hillview)
115	Orchard let to William Bowden (Silveridge, Oaklee)
116	Garden let to William Brown (Vare Oak)
117	Garden let to Samuel Brown (Stile Cottage)
118-19	Higher and Lower Veroak Parks let to Samuel Brown (Oakwood Park & School Playing Field)
120-21	John King's Billageor Village Cross field & Pool Park (part Elmwood Park)
122-25	James Friend's Toopes garden, Long field & Quarry fields (part Elmwood Park)
126-28	Amys (Amos) field, garden and Lower Cross Park let to William Willing (Playing Fields)
131	Harvey's Field (Orchard Terrace and gardens)
132-34	James Friend's fields
135	Orchard (New Churchyard)
136	Lower Poor House field
140-41	James Friend's Park, pasture and homestead.
142	Orchard (Stile Orchard)
187	Thomas Harris's homestead (Great Gate)
188	Barns (Great Gate Barns)
194-95	Feoffees of Slapton's meadow and orchard let to William Denbow
196	Lane (Littlegate lane)
197	Thomas Harris's Well Street meadow
198	Pond
199	Thomas Willing, BUTCHER, Lidstone's orchard

THE DOMESDAY SURVEY

William the Conqueror ordered a survey of his kingdom to be made in 1086. This was to record the size, population and possessions of every parish in order to levy 'geld' (tax). So enumerators arrived and questioned the inhabitants and the results were collated and put into a great Domesday Book.

The Norman Lord of the Manor for Loddiswell at the time was Judhel of Totnes but there is no explanation for William I making him Lord of Totnes and Loddiswell, for little is known of his early life. He must have proved himself to be an able man and have rendered some great service to William to have been entrusted with 107 manors in Devon (as well as one in Cornwall). He set up a motte and bailey castle at Totnes to control the local inhabitants who resented the Norman invasion. The Devon Domesday record sets out details of Loddiswell at that time and reports:

Judhel has a manor called Lodeswilla which Hece held T.R.E. [In the time of Edward the Confessor] and it paid geld for two hides [about 240 acres]. These 12 ploughs can till. Thereof Judhel has one hide and two ploughs in demesne [home farm] and the villeins [farmers] one hide and two ploughs. There Judhel has 20 villeins, 10 bordars [smallholders], six cottagers, eight serfs [slaves with no rights], one rouncey [pack horse], four beasts, six swine, 42 sheep, 11 goats, one fish meadow, half a league of woodland, 13 acres of meadow, half a league of pasture worth 100 shillings when Judhel received the same.

Loddiswell is named as one of the 13 Devon salmon fisheries, paying 30 salmon each year to Judhel. Some of the money gained from Loddiswell taxes was given by him to the Totnes Priory which he founded and which was also supported by a tithe from Loddiswell of swine, sheep, fleeces and cheeses.

POPULATION OF LODDISWELL PARISH

The number of inhabitants in the parish did not vary significantly from the Domesday census of approximately 500 inhabitants, to 1747 when the Rev. Richard Polwhele counted the same number in the census.

W.G. Hoskins' *Devon* gives 608 inhabitants in 1801 and the numbers increased to 1013 by 1841-50. Gradually however, they declined, reaching their lowest of 599 in 1949 and then slowly recovering to 853 in 1996 (an increase which is attributed to the building of new houses and housing estates during that period).

The population of Loddiswell Parish has thus remained reasonably consistent for 1000 years but this masks the changes through that period. Agriculture employed a great number of workers until the gradual mechanisation of agriculture in the 20th century. Families were large with often six to ten children in each household but life expectancy was low due to diseases and epidemics. Advances in medical knowledge were slow until the 20th century and gradually the size of families declined to an average of 2.4 persons per household in the 1990s.

Family structure too has slowly changed during the second half of the 20th century, from the traditional married couples to a significant proportion of households where couples live in partnerships. Some marriages and partnerships have broken down leaving one parent families.

There has also been a national population migration towards the South West of England where the winter climate is milder, and so several people have come to retire in Loddiswell.

This stability in population is in marked contrast to the population of the U.K. as a whole. It is estimated that at the time of the Norman Conquest the total number was about one-and-a-half million. It increased to around five million by 1348-50 when between a quarter and a third of the population was wiped out by the Black Death. Recovery to the five million level took about 100 years to 1450, and over the next 300 years to 1750 the population doubled to about 11 million.

The Industrial Revolution (1750-1850) witnessed a sudden acceleration of technical development, a transfer of the balance of political power from the landowner to the industrial capitalist, and the creation of an organised, industrial working class. The population had again doubled to 22 million and industrial towns and cities developed and expanded.

The 50 million level was reached in 1952 and it is predicted that by the end of the 20th century the population could reach over 70 million. This massive increase in urban dwellers, in contrast to the relatively stable numbers in the rural areas, has brought about environmental pressures on the countryside with a growing demand for rural housing and leisure opportunities.

ARUNDELL CHARITY

After the Norman Conquest, the manor of Hatch in Loddiswell Parish was owned by the Arundells of Sampford in Somerset. The name Arundell is derived from the French word Hirondelle meaning 'swallow' and the family coat-of-arms has six swallows depicted on it. It is possible that the family came from France soon after the Conquest.

After Henry VIII's dissolution of the monasteries (1536-39), Sir Thomas Arundell purchased Slapton Priory and with it the Priory possessions in Loddiswell.

Sir Thomas had become a lawyer in the household of Cardinal Wolsey and he married Margaret Howard, sister to Catherine Howard, and cousin of Anne Boleyn. Both of these ladies became queens of Henry VIII and suffered the fate of execution as did Sir Thomas himself in the following reign of Edward VI.

In 1590 the third wave of the plague swept through the villages of Loddiswell and Stanton, having been brought into the Devon ports by Dutch sailors. Many parishioners died – like the Wyatts of Stanton, for example, who lost four of their family between January and April of that year. It is unknown whether these tragedies influenced Sir Thomas's son Sir Matthew Arundell who was then living at Wardour Castle near Shaftsbury, but in 1591 Sir Matthew made a gift of land and tenements to Loddiswell, the parish of which his family had been so long Lords of the Manor. He founded a charity 'For the use, good and behoof of the parishioners of Loddiswell.'

In 1790 property was described by an indenture to the feoffees:

... all those messuages, lands, tenements and hereditaments called Churchlands situate in Clarke's Heathfield in the Parish of Loddiswell and also a messuage and garden on the east side of the churchyard in Loddiswell and also a messuage called the Church-house or Parish-house, with the common green adjoining thereto, with 16 feet of land, on which a messuage and tenement had been erected and also a messuage, or dwelling house, out-garden and orchard adjoining, containing an acre or thereabouts in the parish of Loddiswell and also an acre of land called Barnwell and also the fourth part of that toft or old pair of walls, called the Lord's Barn or Tye-pit house, all situate in the parish of Loddiswell.

Various grants have been made over the last 400 years. By a deed of 27 January 1872 the feoffees of the Arundell Charity granted to the vicar and churchwardens about a quarter acre of an orchard called the Feoffee Orchard, bounded on the west by the turnpike road, on the north by property of John Came and on the south by a footpath to build a Church School and Headteacher's House.

In 1876 the feoffees gave land on the South side of Stock's Lane, by demolishing the Poor Houses and Gardens for the extension of the Churchyard. The land was consecrated on 7 November 1878.

A water supply was piped from two hydraulic rams at Lower Yanston to a new reservoir at Village Cross, Loddiswell in 1923. The plan was designed by Bob Yabsley and the work was supervised by 'Squire' Eastley, Charge Hand or Works Foreman. The system was maintained by Bill Yabsley,

Engineer, on his return from ship building in Ireland, with his Irish wife and daughter Dolly. The total cost was £1450, the feoffees gave a grant of £425 and undertook to pay £30 per year for 30 years.

By 1927 more space was needed for burials and the feoffees purchased some land on the north side of Stock's Lane from Courthouse, at a cost of £275. A grant was made in 1937 to the newly-formed Nursing Association to provide a resident nurse in the parish.

More recently Arundell Grants have been made to the Loddiswell Playing Fields and Village Hall Trust and for various improvements at the Parish Church.

The farm and other remaining property was sold in 1920 at an auction at the Turk's Head Inn:

Lot 1. Church Cottage sold to Mr J. Hawke for £130.
Lot 2. Gaol Cottage, not sold.
Lot 3. Slated Cottage, sold privately £85.
Lot 4. Garden sold to Mr R. Popplestone for £100.
Lot 5. Barnwell field sold to Mr J. Sparrow for £71.
Lot 6. Churchlands Farm sold to Mr Lethbridge for £1900.
Lot 7. Luke's Tenement sold to Mr J.S. Walke for £1550.

The money was invested in two-and-a-half per cent Consolidated Stock (undated). In 1986 the feoffees were concerned that the capital invested in this stock at 46 per cent had depreciated to 23 per cent of the par value and decided eventually to sell and re-invest the capital in Income Shares with the Charities Official Investment Fund.

The Blackdown Rings were given to the Arundell Charity by the Peek Family of Hazelwood in 1988. The earthworks are considered to be an Iron-Age fortified settlement and the Normans built a fortress in the older earthworks consisting of motte and bailey.

The Loddiswell handbells are held upon trust in perpetuity by the Arundell Charity and include 37 bells covering three complete octaves (25 bells originally belonging to Loddiswell Church were re-tuned and 12 more were added in 1988).

Right: The new churchyard purchased in 1927.

Below: The National Church School and Headmaster's House, built in 1872.

Opposite page: The Poor Houses which were demolished in 1877 to allow for the enlargement of the churchyard.

THE RICHARD PHILIP'S CHARITY

In the Chancel of Loddiswell lies the tomb of Richard Philips of Heathfield who provided for the best-known and most popular of the Loddiswell charities. In 1728 he gave some property to provide income for 'second poor who had, or should not at any time receive any pay or relief of the overseers of the poor'. Anyone who owned a business or property, or even owned a gun and whippet dog for hunting, was not eligible.

Times have changed a lot since then and fortunately we no longer have extreme poverty. The feoffees have, for many years, directed the funds towards senior citizens. In 1997 18 persons between 60 and 70 years received £13 each and 42 persons over 71 years received £15 each.

The distribution takes place yearly on St Stephen's Day (the day after Christmas Day) at 12 noon when a short service is held and the recipients stand on the tomb in the church to receive the money. This tradition still continues. The tomb's inscription reads:

Here lyeth the body of Richard Philips of Heathfield within this parish who departed this life ye 8th. and was buried the 11th. day of April Anno Dom. 1728, in the 68th. year of his age, who by deed bearing date of the 5th. day of the said month gave and pre-sented the fee simple of a messuage and tenement lying in Lupridge to the then feoffees of this parish, their heirs and successors for ever upon trust that they would distribute all the free profits thereof unto the poor of this parish which have no relief, on this tomb, on St. Stephen's Day yearly forever.

The Philips Charity has been administered by the feoffees of the Arundell Charity since 1728. Three members of the Parish Council have been regularly appointed since 1895 to act with the feoffees on this charity.

Right: Feoffee Donald Pethybridge washing the Philips tombstone in the chancel.

Below: The yearly presentation.

LODDISWELL UNION DEATH SOCIETY

The Society was instituted on 25 December 1851 to pay funeral expenses. A subscription of 1 shilling a quarter was collected from members and the funds placed in the Devon & Cornwall Bank in Kingsbridge. The sum of £10 was payable to the member's family on death and during the 19th century this covered all of the funeral expenses. The average rural wage was then about 10 shillings per week and a contribution of 1 shilling a quarter would accumulate to the £10 within 50 years.

The funeral grant remained the same until the Society was wound up in the early 1980s, by which time funeral costs had far exceeded the Society's contribution. The bank balance of around £200 was distributed to the remaining members.

Two of the trustees in the 1930s were Richard West and Jimmy Middlewick, and later William and Walter Hine took over the responsibilities of administration. William's daughter Hilary (Field) remembers being sent with her sister Clarice, to remind members their subscription was due, in order to avoid a fine being imposed by the Society of 6d.

THE CHURCH HOUSE INN

The inn was owned by the Arundell Charity and was situated near the church, backing on to Storridge Lane. James Taylor was the innkeeper in 1778 and his wife took over the lease in 1797 for 99 years. The Taylors – parents and daughter Elizabeth – ran the inn for at least 70 years. Elizabeth died at the age of 89 when James Popplestone, father of Bob, took over until 1867. Aaron Luscombe then became the innkeeper.

On Christmas Eve in 1878, amid the usual festivities, a chimney fire began there and quickly set the thatched roof alight. Sadly the inn was burned down together with the labourer's cottage adjoining, from which George Edgecombe, son of James and Annie, was rescued. Unfortunately the insurance would not cover the cost of rebuilding.

In 1896 Thomas Wyse Weymouth of Woolston House, who had bought part of the adjoining property, tried to build a wall around the site but parishioners pulled it down at night, resulting in a County Court case which he lost. In 1907 Mrs Allin, daughter of Thomas Wyse Weymouth, gave the land to the Church.

The thatched Church House Inn was burnt down in 1878 and the ruins can just be made out in front of the church tower (No. 30 on Tithe Map). The thatched building on the right is the feoffees' parish stable (No. 43 on Tithe Map).

The Courtledge, c.1908.

The Courtledge, 1996.

Chapter 2: Law and Order

Researched by Christian Michell

One of the earliest records of disorder in Loddiswell Parish was found in a 16th-century Star Chamber document (c.1530) which tells of the villainous behaviour of certain riotous young men who came to Ham Farm and caused much distress. It appears that a young man named Honeychurch of Tavistock, but of a very respectable Aveton Gifford family, came with a company of friends to Ham Farm to settle a quarrel by persecuting a blind man called John Phillips and the freeholder of Ham, Christopher Chiswell, and his wife Alysen. The matter had already been settled in the local courts but Honeychurch and 'Co.' were not satisfied with the decision and decided to take the law into their own hands.

Thus began a series of acts of severe persecution. First they drove away from Ham cattle and eight 'melehe kye' by order of Thomas Fortescue, gentleman of Whympstone, Modbury. It was six days before the owners could locate their cattle, which cost them the milk and the time of searching. The young men came again, but this time with 'Wepyns of warre', bows and arrows, swords and daggers, and assaulted the farmer's two sons, who had to defend themselves or they would have been 'utterly slayn and undone'. This time they took away two oxen and held them for three weeks and refused to pay the court order for their mischief Instead they came back to Ham 'as men in furious rage', making another assault on Alysen and the family, who fled indoors for their lives. The gang then took the oxen (it was ploughing time), and three other bullocks 30 miles away. The final indignity was to take newly-washed wool, 120 lbs in weight, and compel poor Chiswell, aged 67, to carry it as far as he was physically able, while poking him with a dagger and shouting 'thief' and 'knave'. In addition, Thomas Fortescue sheared 33 sheep and kept the fleeces.

However, the end of the mischief was in sight. They were caught one day in the act of removing 14 bullocks by John Corbyn, who had arrived with a writ warning Honeychurch to appear in court. The troublemaker was infuriated and drew a sword with which he ran towards Corbyn to slay him, but Corbyn, not being armed, ran through a gap in the hedge, while another of the gang shot an arrow which fortunately missed its target.

One of the others advised Honeychurch to calm down. Alysen, the wife, spoke out too, reminding Honeychurch that he should not behave like that, for after all his father from

Aveton Gifford was a good, law-abiding man and she could not understand how he could be so unneighbourly. Writs were also taken to Thomas Fortescue and others sheltering in his house at Whympstone, Modbury, but they obstinately shut themselves in and would not answer knocks on the door or shouts at the windows, so the writs could not be served upon them.

As they could get no redress the case was brought to the Star Chamber. Unfortunately the result is not known, nor will ever be known until the second document is discovered.

Many years later in 1749 the parishioners of Loddiswell drew up an agreement to help protect each other from burglary and felony and to jointly recompense any of their losses.

One of the duties of the Annual Vestry Meeting was to appoint the parish constables whose responsibility it was to keep order or arrest any offenders and put them in the pillory or stocks. This was probably at the end of the Courtledge near Stocks Lane. Robert Popplestone, the carpenter, was instructed to make a pair of stocks in 1823 and they are now kept in the church (*above*).

The *Western Daily Mercury* reported that in 1840:

... a boy was found fighting in the Church on the Sabbath Day. He was put in the stocks by order of the Rector, and released a few hours later after an apology. His Mother came with a hatchet, not to harm anyone, but threatened to cut her son free.

The stocks were later kept in the jail which William Kennard, a weaver, rented from the feoffees. They reserved the right to have free use of a room as stated in the indenture:

A room to putt place and keep a pair of stocks, with free ingress, egress and regress, to make use of them for punishing or safe keeping of any malefactor, and power at all times to hold and keep their courts in the same building.

In 1720 William Kennard was paid ls.10d. for keeping a man under guard and in 1723 he was paid £1.2s.7d. 'for the charges on the guard', this enormous sum possibly being incurred by poachers ignoring the stricter Game Laws.

Robert Hyne was paid ls.6d. for riding to North Huish 'about Whitelock' and the following year (1725), 'Expense for carrying Whitelock to Exeter 17s.6d. – Paid for three horses to ride to Exeter 15s.6d., Robert Hyne for four days and Rich Burn three days to carry Whitelock to Exeter, and Robert Hyne 4s.6d. for what he paid the guardsman for keeping Whitelock'.

By 1817 the cottage was no longer a jail but was used for poor persons supported by the parish.

THE POUND

Loddiswell had a parish pound in a square between Prospect, Virginia and Whitelock's cottages. Pounds were where straying animals were impounded and, as in Loddiswell, were usually near the church. Once an animal was impounded, the owner had to pay a fee for its release, so naturally this made people more careful about fencing in their livestock. In the last century it was usual for cottagers to keep a pig, and some of these did escape and stray on the roads.

In 1860 Leah Luscombe was coming out of church one Sunday and was incensed to see P.C. Chudleigh driving her father's two pigs towards the pound. Leah was a lady of action. She intercepted the pigs and despite having just come from church in her best clothes, rescued the pigs before they were locked up.

That was not the end of the matter. P.C. Chudleigh took her to court on a charge of rescuing two pigs whilst in police custody. Leah spoke up, Yes, she had caught her father's pigs before they were put in the pound, and as not one foot was put inside the pound she did not consider it was necessary to pay a fee for caring for the animals.

Then her father was heard. Obviously he recalled that one of the family had already been caught by P.C. Chudleigh and there was every reason to be angry with the policeman. He told the magistrates that he had seen his pigs safe in the court at his house before leaving for church and hinted that P.C. Chudleigh was a very vindictive man. He firmly believed that the constable himself had let out his pigs and taken them to the pound in revenge. P.C. Chudleigh stoutly denied this and said Luscombe's pigs were constantly on the roads.

Fortunately for Leah and her father there were no eye-witnesses – everybody had been attending church when the pigs took their illegal stroll round Courtledge. The charge was withdrawn, but Luscombe had to pay the costs. This was not entirely a victory for the owner, for they would have been considerable; in 1862, for example, four boys were summoned for playing football on the highroad and were fined 6d. with 7 shillings costs. In the same year a father who incited his son to steal two mangolds spent three weeks in prison and a man who stole 30 apples was sentenced to 21 days' hard labour.

Granny Hine's and Jail Cottage, 1900.

COURTLEDGE AND TYEPITTE

The property given to the Arundell Charity in 1591 included 'the Church House Inn, the Common Green, and the fourth part of an old pair of walls called the Lord's Barn or Tye-pit [now Tyepitte] House'. It is clear that the old Tithe Barn originally stood in this area to store the fleeces, cheeses and other produce due to the Church as tithes or 'tenths' for the Priory at Totnes. This would have been before 1413 when the College of Slapton took over the Rectorial rights of Loddiswell. In *Stafford's Register* it was recorded that the Vicarage was between the villages of Staunton and Loddiswell (i.e. Femhill House) and that there were 'barns lately built there for storing crops and receiving wool, corn and animals as tithes'.

The name Tyepitte also refers to one of the three sawpits in the Courtledge area. Before the days of the circular saw a tree was hauled along the top of a pit, about 7 feet deep, and two men would saw planks with a long, double-ended crosscut saw. The man in the pit had the easiest, though dirtiest, job of pulling the saw down while the skilled man on top had to guide the direction and the depth of the cut.

In front of Tyepitte House and cottages there was a trap house and yard for logs and faggots, with the area being defined by a border of pitching stones. William Henry Elliott was asked in 1971 to describe that end of the Courtledge when he was a boy. He said:

I was born on the 26th day of November 1878 in Loddiswell. For the first nine or ten years of my life I lived at Tyepitte House with my father William Elliott, my mother Selina Elliott and my maternal grandmother by name Mary Ann Lugger who was the owner of Tyepitte House and also the three cottages and gardens known as Tyepitte Cottages.

In about the year 1889 my father bought the bakery business at 10 Fore Sweet, Loddiswell and our household moved to the Bakery. I continued however to visit my grandmother Mary Ann Lugger until she died on 17 April, 1907. I very clearly remember the ground on the south side of Tyepitte House. There were standing on it woodricks and a linhey around which I used to play as a child. At the south-western corner of the property there was

an old wooden pump which was fastened to an ash tree growing beside it with two pieces of wood to prevent it tipping over. Beside the pump on the side away from the cottages was a stone trough about 6 feet long. To the east of the lower end of the trough were two pitching stones... far enough away from the pump to permit a pony and trap to drive between them and the pump. Beside these pitching stones was a wooden linhay some 9 or 10 feet wide and about 20 feet long. This linhay had double doors facing in the direction of Tyepitte House. Each of the doors was broad enough for a trap to drive in but my father used the building for the storing of wood. The roof of this linhay was thatched on the top with bundles of furze which followed the shape of the roof.

At the back of the linhay was one of a pair of clothes posts, the other being in front of Tyepitte House where there were two more pitching stones. Beside the linhay my father often placed a faggot rick running up from the linhay towards Tyepitte House. Sometimes my father would bring home a wagon load of hardwood. He would tip this beside the faggot rick preparatory to sawing it up and splitting it with a biddle and wedges and packing it into the linhay.

Thatched Tyepitte House with the clothes posts showing to the right.

The clothes line was the subject of discussion by the Parish Council in 1907, the year that Mary Ann Lugger died. Col. Wise moved a resolution 'that the Kingsbridge District Council have their attention called to certain obstacles near the highway in the Courtledge with a view to the removal of the same'.

Now Mary Ann Lugger, or 'Granny Lugger' as the family knew her, had been rather outspoken. One day, when the Colonel was riding his hunter down through the Church School ground and across to Court House he was annoyed by the clothes drying on the line and said to Granny Lugger 'One of these days I will hurt my nose on your clothes line'. She replied 'Yes sir, people with big noses had better look after them't'.

For many years the Courtledge has been the place where carnivals have begun and where the celebrations of royal and national occasions have been held. In 1988 the Parish Council, in full discussion with the public at meetings in the Village Hall and in co-operation with South Hams District Council and Devon County Highways Dept, redesigned the lay-out of the whole Courtledge area.

View of Courtledge and Prospect Cottages from the 'Central Cross'.

Thatched Jail House Cottage (in the centre of the photo), c.1910.

Chapter 3: Parish Council

Before considering the role of the 20th-century Parish Councils it is worth looking behind the scenes to see what preceded them. Towards the end of the reign of Elizabeth I in 1601, overseers of the poor were instituted by an Act of Parliament and each parish had laid on it the duty of feeding its own needy parishioners. The term 'guardians' was not used until 1735.

About 1589 a certain number of parishioners met at intervals in the parish vestry for the dispatch of parochial business and in 1672 this body was given legal status, becoming known as 'Parish Vestry'. They collected three rates – poor, church and ways. One or two of their number were appointed as waywardens who were responsible for the repair of the byways, bridges and roadside ditches. The Highway Rate was partially relieved when, in 1823, the Turnpike Trust was formed to improve some of the main South Hams road network.

The Parish Vestry were managers of the parish workhouse wherever one existed, but the nearest to Loddiswell was at Kingsbridge Union Road where those with no means of financial support were sent. A few families slightly better off financially were housed in the village Poor Houses situated to the east of the church and, later, in the Jail House when it was no longer needed for miscreants.

The payment of a 'Church Rate' agreed by the Vestry, was compulsory until the 1880s when Gladstone's government made it optional. This funding was taken on by the Church Commissioners, in due course administered through their Diocesan Boards of Finance. The Parish Vestry continued to function until the birth of the Parish Councils in 1894.

Loddiswell Parish Council met on 4 December 1894 in the National School Room when the first councillors were elected, and soon after settled down to the business of acquiring a box 'for the purpose of keeping the books, etc. in, belonging to the Council'. Enquiries were made to the County Council as to the custody of the Parish Tithe Map which the vicar objected to giving up. Diplomatically it was agreed that it should be transferred to the custody of the Parish Council,

'kept in the Vestry under lock and key, and the key kept in the charge of the Clerk'.

The more important business of the Council involved the acquisition and allocation of a lease of land suitable for allotments. Kingsbridge Local Committee on Technical Education offered to give instruction to the 'Parish in Practical Gardening and any Agricultural Process which may be deemed to be of most use to the Rural District'. The water supplies in Well Street, Hal's Well, and the Courtledge pump, needed constant attention and footpaths, particularly at Littlegate, were in need of improvements.

The overseers of the poor of the parish were responsible for the collection of the rates until 1926, and from 1927 this responsibility was undertaken by the Rating Authority of the Rural District Council. Two overseers were appointed until 1926 at the Annual Parish Meeting, to verify assessments but it was the duty of an assistant overseer to draw up a valuation list of properties in the parish and appropriate their rates. He then visited every house and farm in the parish twice yearly, to collect the rates due, and for this he received a salary of around £22 per annum. The last assistant overseer and rate collector was Trowbridge Horton (*above*), whose family still live at Vine House in Towns Lane.

A Demand Note for a half year in 1925 shows the purposes for which the rates were used:

Relief of the Poor and other expenses of the
Guardians – Five & a halfpence General
Expenses of Rural Council (including highways)
Sanitary General – One shilling, six pence
General County Purposes (including General
Education) – Two shillings, five & three-quarter
pence
Expenses of the Overseers and Parish Council – Nine
& three quarter pence
Total – Five shillings, three pence

When the Rural District Council were responsible for rate collection from 1927 a Rating Authority was formed, with two representatives from each parish in the Rural District, the first two from Loddiswell being Mr Philip Brooks of Woolston Farm and Mr L.R. Sampson of Tunley Farm.

The Mains electricity was first brought to Loddiswell in 1928/29 and Owen Elliot remembers Tyepitte House being wired by Fred Crabb, a Loddiswell electrician who worked for Paul Pinch of Totnes. A mains link from Loddiswell to Modbury was erected in the mid 1930s and a branch from Yanston to Woolston House in 1938.

The need for street lighting was raised in 1952 and an estimate was obtained from the South West Electricity Board of £360 for installing 11 lights. After a lengthy discussion it was agreed that the cost was extremely high and that the resolution of January 1952 'that a public meeting be held in order to adopt Street Lighting and the Watching Act of 1833' should be rescinded.

A new scheme was considered in 1955 when the cost would be £90 to £100 as opposed to the £360 quoted three years earlier. The reason for this lay in the fact that where overhead wiring existed the actual wiring would be paid for by the Board but three years before, the Council concerned had to bear all the cost. The first 11 lamps installed were to be at Little Gate, New Bridge Inn, Town's Lane, Ashwood Park, Oakwood Park, Court House, Pointridge and Corner House, with the remainder to be sited following discussion with the Board.

Local Government was re-organised in 1974 and new District Councils came into power on 1 April. Rural and urban District Councils, such as Kingsbridge and Salcombe, became Parish Councils but were given the option to be known as 'Town Councils' and name their Chairman as 'Town Mayor'. Their duties and powers were to be the same as Parish Councils and the existing Parish Councils remained intact. Loddiswell and surrounding parishes are represented on the new South Hams District Council whose offices are at Follaton House in Totnes.

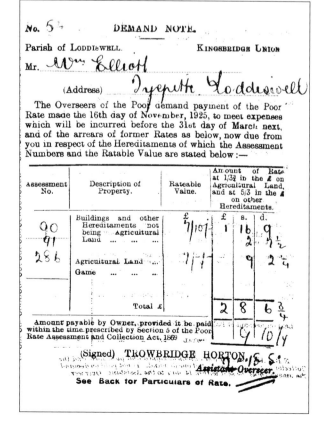

Over the years, the Loddiswell Parish Council has influenced planning decisions, particularly since 1950 when 'ribbon development' was deemed undesirable. Transport and traffic had generally increased and cul-de-sac and residential estates gave more privacy and less disturbance. In Loddiswell there have been several residential developments at different times, encouraged by the Parish Council in order to ensure the existence of village shops and churches, and a public house and school. Street lighting, car parking, and public toilets have been provided by the Parish with help from the District Council and other authorities. The most recent project was the construction of a bus shelter in the village centre.

Top: Manuella Lynn-Bertoli became Loddiswell's street cleaner in 1998.

Left: A rates demand note made out by Trowbridge Horton.

Below: The bus shelter built in 1998.

Chapter 4: Footpaths in Loddiswell

Walking in the countryside is one of Britain's most popular recreational activities. There are 120 000 miles of public rights of way in our country and these paths are home to all sorts of country life. They also help maintain the rural character, and provide a valuable means of enjoying life outdoors away from the motor vehicle.

Loddiswell has 13 public footpaths covering over four-and-a-half miles, and three disused roads now used as paths. The Definitive Map of the Parish which was drawn up in 1950 registers all these paths. Five of them are within the village boundaries, and mainly form convenient short-cuts, well used in bygone days and still popular today.

F.P.11 is a short path which begins in Well Street, crosses a meadow, passes the Vicarage and joins the B3196 at Little Gate. F.P.12 – known by the locals as 'Inkly-Crinkly' – starts at its junction with F.P.11 near Little Gate, drops into a little valley, climbs up the other side, mounts several steps and emerges in Station Road near Torr View.

The short F.P.2 runs from the Courtledge, past the Village Hall to the B3196, where F.P.5 begins next to Stile Cottage. This path continues through Elmwood Park, alongside the school field and on to Clarke's Barn Road. F.P.6 then takes up the journey at a stile and crosses pasture fields eventually exiting on to an unclassified road 200 yards east of Higher Yanston.

Step outside the village and our footpaths wind through the countryside, rich with wild flowers, animals and birds. People are drawn from all walks of life to relax and enjoy a breath of rural air. Silveridge Lane, F.P.4, is located off the B3196 about 200 yards north of Ham Farm. This narrow path bordered on each side by long-established hedges, offers glimpses of glorious, undulating countryside. The path steepens and winds its way down to the River Avon where it joins F.P.19. It meanders through Silveridge Woods and alongside the river beneath a canopy of trees, where in springtime, daffodils and primroses peep between the undergrowth. They are followed by a carpet of bluebells which herald the arrival of summer. This path crosses bridges and stiles alongside the river

and then veers off towards Reads Farm where it joins the County road.

Wigford Lane is situated approximately 170 yards north east of Wigford Farm. This path, F.P. 17, winds its way down beside mixed woodlands, through a pine wood, past Topsham Cottages and joins the County road near Topsham Bridge, a local beauty spot. From here walkers can follow F.P.3 to Crannacombe Farm, beginning the journey beside the river, over the old rail track and through a kissing gate. The path winds through an ash plantation, crosses a stream, then runs alongside a wooded area next to the River Avon until it passes through a gate for a very steep assent to where it joins the lane near Cranna-combe Farm.

Sue Sweeney, waymarking the footpaths, 1998.

At the western side of the village is F.P.15, which begins near Higher Greystones Farm. The path crosses arable and pasture land, through gates and over stiles and offers extensive views of the beautiful Avon Valley. The path eventually joins Greenlands Head Lane which leads down to Hatch Bridge. Another path, F.P.16, can be picked up here alongside the River Avon but walkers can only proceed a short distance before having to back-track as there is no exit to the path.

Although Loddiswell has no bridleways, Greenlands Head Lane, Great Gate to New Mill, and Ham Butts to Mill Hill are all disused roads, popular with riders and walkers alike. In 1995 Loddiswell Parish Council joined the Parish Paths Partnership Scheme with Devon County Council, whereby the parish receives a yearly sum of money to maintain and repair the footpaths. The scheme is operated by Sue Sweeney (*above*) for the Parish Council and since its introduction much work has been carried out on the paths in the parish. They are surveyed each year, trimmed where necessary and any broken stiles replaced. With the help and co-operation of the landowners much has been done to improve the surfaces, waymark the routes and draw attention to their existence.

The ongoing programme of work will help us all to appreciate the beauty of our rural landscapes and help us to respect the life and work which continues here throughout the changing seasons.

Hillside and The Manse, c.1900 before Hillside was re-built and slated by Harry Rundle's father, John.

Thatched cottage in Town's Lane and (inset) Gladys and Dick Perring in Town's Lane.

Chapter 5: Houses in Loddiswell

The old houses in the village were mainly thatched until about 1850 but by 1990 there were only three; Jubilee Cottage (formerly the Jail House), Little Gate at the south end of the village (*right*) and The Cottage, Town's Lane.

The older terraced houses in Well Sweet and Town's Lane were thatched and built partially of cob. The Church House Inn and a group of houses between the Pound and Well Sweet were also thatched. In April 1864 a fire broke out in the blacksmith's shop near Virginia Cottage and raged through the five cottages below. Four belonged to Thomas Willing, a butcher of Little Reads, who was not insured. The Local Authority stipulated that any new buildings must be covered with slate and no thatch was to be used. The fire contributed to the death of the Blacksmith's son who had been ill and the event had a significant effect on the community; at a Vestry meeting, the Rev. Chalk suggested that a fire brigade be formed. It would appear that the fire engine was a necessity for in 1871 a thatched cottage in a row of three caught fire. The villages stripped the roof of thatch, and water was poured freely on the flames, saving the three houses.

Another local disaster occurred in 1917, when Heath Farmhouse burned down. Mrs Yalland, of the village shop, hastened towards Heath to help her friends, the Ellis Family. In the narrow lanes she was forced to keep running in front of the fire

Above left: Heath Farm where the thatch caught fire in 1917 and the fire brigade had to be called out.
Above: Wyselands Farm House.

Above: Stile Cottage where the stage coach horses could be changed on their journey to Wrangaton. The barn on the left housed the horse-drawn fire engine (left).

Below: Silveridge House and the Handy Shop, formerly Sydney and Winnie Jeffery's watch repairs hardware shop, 1944-88.

brigade until she came to a gate way where the horses could pass her. The fire engine was kept in the barn near Stile Cottage.

A few large houses were built between 1880 and 1910. Harvey Villa, as the name suggests, was built for Richard Harvey in about 1890 and John Yalland moved there after selling the London House Stores to Reginald Ward in 1929. John's wife Louise was Cornish and named the house Gorran and it was not until Alfred Hingston retired from Ham Farm that it was renamed Silveridge.

Pointridge was a field on the 1839 Tithe Map and by 1906 the Rates Book records that the house, garden and buildings there were owned and occupied by Jasper Yalland Junr.

Chevithorne, on the southern boundary of the village, was built in 1910 for John Tapp, the retiring National School headmaster.

Tyepitte House was rebuilt in 1910 by Bob Yabsley for William Elliott, the baker.

Housing legislation in Britain began with the Artisans' Dwellings Act of 1875 which gave powers to local councils to condemn properties and clear slums within their boundaries. The Housing of the 1890 Working Classes Act strengthened earlier

Right: Pointridge with the Blacksmith's shop to the right.

Below: This very old and poor photo shows the pump which supplied water to the Courtledge area. The old Tyepitte House was thatched, 1905.

Acts and encouraged local councils to undertake housing improvement schemes. Under an Act of 1919 the government offered a subsidy for houses built by a local council for rent.

The first council houses in Loddiswell were in New Road where six were built in 1927/28 to re-house families from the deteriorating terraced houses in Quarry Park (later renamed Station Road). The Clerk of the Parish Council wrote to the District Council in March 1939 pointing out the urgent need for houses, taking into consideration the large number of houses being condemned under the New Slum Clearance Scheme. Many of these houses were built partly of cob with no indoor sanitation or water. The water closet (WC) or earth closet was either outside the back door or at the bottom of the garden and water was fetched from the nearest communal pump or well.

During the Second World War all residential building work was suspended and materials were used to temporarily repair or shore up town and city buildings after bomb damage. Many young people at the end of the war decided to marry and the housing needs of the area were desperate. Young couples quite often had no alternative but to live with their parents and consideration was given to the building of council housing estates.

Four prefabricated bungalows (prefabs) were erected in Oakwood Park in 1946 and plans were drawn up for ten council houses in Ashwood Park. Building materials were very scarce but the first houses were completed in 1947. They were quite large family houses all of a similar design with back gardens and a common grass frontage. Very little thought was given to car parking then and in later years parking spaces were provided within the grassland area. A further 20 houses were built in 1951/52 and this accommodated the most urgent needs. Street lights had been discussed for many years and in 1955 the first 11 were installed.

A group of four council houses were built in 1955 at the north end of the parish near California Cross. Russell and Jean Baker occupied No.1. as it was close to their engineering workshop, later to become California Cross Service Station. In 1960 Bungalows for single and retired couples were constructed at Ashwood Close along a pathway leading from Ashwood Park.

The District Council has followed Government policy since 1960 allowing tenants to buy their council houses after a few years of residence. This was encouraged by the 'Right to Buy' Acts of 1979 and 1985.

A flurry of activity occurred in 1964/65 when the District Council cleared the old Pitt Cottages and built the first of 11 flats at Pitt Court. In 1964 a new initiative for private development appeared in order to satisfy the demand for more houses and 24 bungalows were constructed in a pleasant cul-de-sac at Town's Park overlooking the Avon Valley, half of them immediately being bought by couples who were working in the district. The District Council, too, was aware of the need for flats and bungalows, partly to re-accommodate couples from the larger council houses whose families had grown up. A prize-winning layout was fitted in at Arundell Place in 1968 utilising the garden areas behind the terraced houses of Fore Street with access near the Congregational Church.

The site at Oakwood Park became derelict as the prefabs, built in 1946, had outlived their usefulness by 1966 and three were removed to Reads Farm in 1968 to form piggeries and a workshop. Ivor and Joan King acquired a site to build Vare Oak in 1971 but the area behind in Oakwood

Above: Cross House and Cross Farm.
Top: The first council houses in New Road built in 1927/28.

Park was not developed until 1979. It was bought by Bert Taylor and his colleague under the name of their partnership Taylor and Toms, and seven dwellings were built.

A Loddiswell Development Plan was drawn up in 1975 and Phase One was implemented. Building began in Elmwood Park and the first 31 houses were occupied by October 1978, while six more bungalows were being constructed. The Parish Council influenced the design of this private development by suggesting that instead of an estate of bungalows and gardens, the approach should have terraced houses in keeping with the main streets of the village. It was recommended that bungalows should be built at the higher elevations to protect the appearance of the skyline and the remainder should be a mix of flats, bungalows, and two-, three- and four-bedroom houses. It would provide an opportunity for retired grandparents to live near their families and thus a desirable intermix of the community. The

demand for these houses encouraged the developers to build another 44 in the second phase.

A few smaller groups of houses were erected privately between 1978 and 1998: at Stile Orchard in Well Street, near the site of the old blacksmith's shop, at Little Gate, Aswell Orchard and in New Bridge gardens.

In-filling by private development has continued during the second half of the 20th century in Well Street, Station Road, Town's Lane and Village Cross Road.

From the 1960s to the '90s some farmers in the countryside were granted planning permission for a bungalow to house staff, or to retire into, but by the 1990s many farm buildings were redundant, being unsuitable for modern farming methods and they were converted for residential use. Great Gate Barns, Wyseland Barn, Higher Hazelwood, Crannacombe, Hown and Stanton Barns are typical examples where the traditional stonework has been retained.

Above: Stile Orchard and Well Street.
Top: Aerial view of New Road houses (in the foreground), the chapel and school and the development of Arundell Place, 1970.

Well Street in the days before the thatched building in the background was slated for Fred Kernick's blacksmith's shop.

Old Fore Street and the bank.

Fore Street and the bank, 1901.

The Old Vicarage

The *Post Office Directory* of 1873 states: The Vicarage House was greatly enlarged and indeed rebuilt in 1865, and is a most commodious and elegant residence, beautifully situated about three-quarters of a mile from the village, and within ten minutes' walk of Woolston and Alleron which, with Hazelwood, the residence of William Peek Esq., constitutes the principal houses in the parish.

Stafford's Register in 1413 refers to land and the Rector's Manse situated between Staunton and Loddiswell, together with barns lately built there for storing crops and receiving wool, corn and animals as tithes.

The old vicarage was described in detail in a terrier of the Loddiswell Parish in 1683 and in total there were ten under-rooms, one staircase, eight chambers, four cock-loft chambers, seven chimneys and two ovens. A close court 27 foot square and an open court adjoined outhouses, two barns, a stable and a cider pound.

Plans for the present dwelling house were drawn up in 1865 and it was built in 1868. It was well established when the Rev. Henry Townend lived there in 1878 and it was the vicarage for the Reverends Boultbee, Hodges, Gane and George Bliss until the living was merged with Woodleigh in 1955 (by which time the glebelands had already been sold). The Vicarage House is now called Fernhill House and is the home of Michael and Carolyn Winterton.

The Rev. Henry Townsend outside Loddiswell Vicarage, 1870.

Hazelwood House (Hals Wood)

Richard Peek bought the property from Anderson Morshead in 1827 as it had a pleasant view over the beautiful Avon Valley. The house was in a poor state of repair and in 1830 Richard had it rebuilt, planning, in due course, to retire there. He was elected High Sheriff of London in 1832 and soon after returned to live in the parish. Building work on the estate continued and several lodges, a chapel, stables and out-houses were built with each boundary wall incorporating a unique design of recesses and cappings.

Richard invited Sunday School children, their teachers and the general public to special treats each July during his lifetime and through the years the estate has provided the venue for meets of the hunting fraternity, for cricket on a pitch in the meadow land and for many other events.

The house in 1990 (left) after enlargement in 1913 and 1920 and complete with its thatch, c.1850 (below).

Woolston House

The older ordnance maps of the area refer to 'the site of an ancient mansion' situated just south of Woolston Farmstead. It was the Manor House of Webbeton and in 1676 was listed among the 'High Rents' because of the various tenements owned, including: 'Woodrew Moore, Crannacombe, Coomb, Topsham, Rewton (Reveton) and Staunton Moore'. Further east from the Manor House towards the main Loddiswell to Wrangaton road were Webbeton Cottages.

Some time before the end of the 17th century a new residence was built on adjoining land and in the 1747 *History of Devon*, Polwhele described Woolston as 'a handsome modern building situated about a mile from the town, the residence of George Furlong Wise Esqr.' About 18 acres of farmland was enclosed to provide a walled garden, shrubbery, lawns and parkland. Rev. Charles Foulkes Osmond married Caroline Jane Wise, the heiress of the property, and in the mid

1840s built a lodge and new driveway. Beech trees were planted on each side and it was about this time that a belt of trees was planted around the parkland. Thomas Wyse Weymouth, a Kingsbridge solicitor, bought the estate, including the house, Woolston Farm, Stanton Farm and village in 1871 and his granddaughters Elfrida Gladys Conran and Winifred Evelyn Allin eventually inherited the property. They retained the house until selling in 1938.

Horse and four-wheeled carriage at Woolston House, the home of Thomas Wyse Weymouth, 1890.
Top: Woolston Lodge, built in 1845 (photographed 1997).

Alleron

The old farmhouse was owned in 1515 by the Kings who sold to the Wise Family in the late 1700s. The Regency part of the house was added in about 1816 and a stone butter house was built in the front garden, positioned over a cool spring. The lead spout which leads into a lily pond is dated 1818. A large thatched barn was in a ruinous condition in 1975 and has since been demolished. There is a round, walled garden with a diameter of 88 feet built with stone and cob to a height of 8 feet and it was re-thatched in 1970 to keep the cob dry. A stream was diverted by the Wise family to supply water to the garden and additional space for vegetables was provided outside, enclosed by a circular earth bank on three sides. The only other round garden believed to exist in England is in Warwickshire.

Charles Dacres Wise retired from the Colonial Office in Rhodesia and came to live there in the late 1920s. He was actively involved in the Management of Loddiswell Primary School and with a number of other parish affairs for many years. The property passed to his daughters Stella and Betty Wise in 1951 and it was sold to the Parish family in 1952.

Alleron House, 1940.

Hatch Arundell

The *Post Office Directory* of 1873 omitted reference to Hatch Arundell except to state that Robert Martin, farmer, lived there. It is probably the oldest of the principal houses and was shown on all of the old maps – Saxton's 1577, John Speed's 1611, Johan Blaeu 1648, John Morden 1695, R. Blome 1673, on the 18th-century Bowden, Bowles, Kitchen and Haywood, and the finest of all, Benjamin Donn's of 1765.

Hatch (alternatives are Hache, Hecce and Hax) must have been pioneered and settled by a West-Saxon tribal family soon after AD700, when, having surged across the Exe, they came looking not for conquest but for land to farm. Their labours were

rewarded, for after 200 years the manor seems roughly to have embraced a good part of what is now Loddiswell Parish. After the Conquest it was King John who divided it into two – Hatch Manor and Loddiswell, both then of course with Norman overlords. As both were called 'Lord of the Manor of Loddiswell' concurrently, it can lead to some confusion.

John de Arundell seems to have been the earliest of the medieval owners to have left his name permanently here. Later, Thomas Gyll successfully petitioned King Edward IV for a licence to castellate the house and to enclose parkland, and has left his coat of arms in glass in the parish church.

All of this lies in the shadows of the distant past and it is perhaps best to read the story as unfolded by Alan Saville of Hatch Arundell, the present owner, who writes:

Not until Tudor times do these shadows come into focus a little, when the generations of Carswell assume the shape of people we can recognise, but in the Stuart parliaments Sir John Eliot steps upon a national stage in a blaze of fame. Having played out his splendid part he withdraws, and his death in the Tower leads directly to the present partition of the estate into Higher and Lower Hatch Arundell.

His Puritan kinsfolk the Langworthys are left to sustain throughout the rest of that century of ferment, the perilous but not undignified role of dissenter landowner. The Hanoverian era sees prominent Puritan squire yield to anonymous Georgian gentleman and the climax has passed.

The succeeding name, that of Prideaux, is again one of the very ancient lineage but in the changing times and with diminishing resources the owner of Hatch Arundell no longer wielded power. 'Lord of the Manor' had dwindled to a courtesy title with very minor advantages, and when Corn Laws were no more, and Free Trade ruined agriculture, effective local or political influence left these acres for ever.

The narrator of this pageant is sharply conscious of having rung down the final curtain with two heavily symbolic acts. It fell to him to commute the last tithe paid here, thus interring one of the most venerable institutions of the Realm, and secondly he was the first owner of this house never to have had any land to farm. A chain as old as England had snapped and only the name and the ghosts remain.

Chapter 6: A Photographic Portrait of Field Sports in the Parish

Hunting

Above: Modbury Harriers meet at Hazelwood, 1933.
Left: South Pool Harriers meet at Hatch Arundell, 1992.
Below: Lawn meet at Woolston House, 1900.

Shooting, Ferreting and Badger Digging

Above: Ferreting was the traditional Boxing Day activity before myxomatosis devastated the rabbit population. Harold Lethbridge keeps a few ferrets for the occasional day's rabbiting and for competing in events at village and agricultural shows.

Above: Pheasant shoot at Hazelwood, 1937.
Left to right: George Stephens, Andrew Halliday, John Welch-Thornton, Roger Peek, Charles D. Wise, William Peek.

Above: A well-attended group of Loddiswell badger diggers and spectators beside the River Avon, 12 April 1923.

Chapter 7: St Michael and All Angels

There was a church in Loddiswell earlier than 1088; but in that year Judhel was Lord of the Manor. He held many manors including Totnes and had taken Loddiswell when the Normans dispensed with Hecce the Saxon Lord.

Judhel the Norman Lord gave Totnes a priory and the foundation deed describes the enactment of this gift. 'Judhel presented the key, the bell rope and his own dagger to a monk in the name of Tetbald.' Not only did Judhel give the Priory to Totnes but he endowed it with yearly gifts from some of the other manors. The deed states 'Likewise from Churcheton in Lodevilla the half (of the tithe) on the year's increase and of the churches, and the whole tithe of all movable things, swine, sheep, fleeces, cheeses, etc.' Loddiswell paid Totnes Priory yearly up to the time of the dissolution when the sum of 6s.8d. was paid.

The first recorded rector is Walter de Lodeswell in 1250 who rebelled against paying the yearly tax to Totnes Priory. Some 190 years had elapsed since that foundation deed had been signed and in 1280 Walter de Loddiswell was accused of not honouring the agreement, and had not paid the dues to Totnes. Walter the rector was legally in the wrong and it seems that a suit would be brought before the Dean of Exeter. Walter would have to answer to a higher authority, which would not have been palatable, for this was by no means the first of his transgressions. So it was, that on Wednesday before the feast of St Barnabas 1280 (11 June) at Loddiswell the rector agreed to pay the tithe and appended his seal. This deed was signed by Lord Radulphus de Cheverstone, knight Lord Willelmus de Cheverstone, knight. William Crispin, knight, Robertus de Mallestone, Johannes de Newetone and others. This is perhaps the first documentary record of objection to the local taxation and may arouse some sympathy from modern ratepayers.

In the following year another Priory deed records happenings at Loddiswell. Andrew de Lodeswille, chaplain, for the sum of five silver marks yearly was leased all tithes from the parish of Alfincton, from Rake, Alynstone, Edeltonne, Portemus and Sure. The tithes were called 'Seynte Mariedole'.

John Wyecliffe was rector from 1391 to 1405. His will tells us that he asked Rob Frenche to help his executors when they came to Devon. He left money to Woodleigh, Churchstow, Dodbrooke, Thurlestone, Bigbury and Aveton Gifford churches but no mention of Loddiswell. He did leave ten marks for his poor parishioners for bread and shoes. There was a touching bequest in that will 'To Bob Frenche his wine bottles, a silver cup (and cover) to drink wine in, and 100 shillings to buy himself wine, because testator could no longer drink wine with him (unless God so wills)'. The other major sum of 100 shillings was to John Meryk to pray for his soul.

RECTORS TO 1405

1258	Walter de Lodeswell
1262	Andrew de Lodeswell
1265	William de Lodeswell
1282-3	William de la Haye
1309	Peter de Hellewille
1317	Nicholas de Arundelle
1328	Master John le Zouche
1343	Sir Richard Mulso
1350	Sir John de Horncastre
	Sir William Markere
1391	John Whytloffe
1405	Thomas la Zouche

In 1413 the College of Slapton made what can be described as a 'takeover bid' for the Rectory of Loddiswell. The Bishop summoned the interested parties including Loddiswell's rector to meet at Clyst. Slapton certainly needed the money to continue its work, so it was decided that the fruits of Loddiswell's Rectory (from tithes), should be divided between Slapton and Loddiswell, the rectorial rights to belong to Slapton Chantry and a vicar to be installed here. *Stafford's Register* spells out exactly the terms of the appropriation. Land, barns and the rector's manse were then between the villages of Stanton and Loddiswell in the area of Femhill House. Slapton was to have the tithes of the whole parish, together with barns lately built there for storing crops and receiving wool, corn and animals as tithes.

The rector Peter Holdych was to be the first vicar. He was given a pension of 20 shillings per annum (a disturbance fee) and also a salary of 50 shillings per annum. Holdych, now vicar, was responsible for paying Totnes Priory their pension of 6s.8d. per year. The new vicar was also responsible for Buckland-Tout-Saints and was to 'Preach one sermon a month in the chappell'. A terrier dated 1683 mentions that the vicar had a riding way over a field called Ryder's, and that if 'The said field be in tillage the vicar is to have a key to the gates for his free passage.'

Vicars of Loddiswell

VICARS, 1935-99

Left to right from top: George Alfred Bliss A.K.C. H.C.F. (1935-55), Wilfred H. G. Summerell, rector of Loddiswell and Woodleigh (1955-68), William Stanley Tyler, rector of Loddiswell and Woodleigh (1968-77), Dr Robert J.K. Law, rector of Loddiswell, Woodleigh, Morleigh and Halwell (1977-94), Roderick David Withnell, vicar of Loddiswell, Woodleigh and East Allington (1994-).

VICARS 1413 TO 1643

1413	Peter Holdych
1435	Sir William Bowrynge
1439	Master Benedict Brente
1440	Sir William Bowrynge
1462	Richard Burleigh
1468	William Bickley
	William Prickett
1502	Andrew Cope
1502	Robert Smyth
1504	Nicholas Morton
1517	Richard Prust
1558	John Forde. M.A.
1573	Richard Fountayne
1599	Clement Ellis
1637	Edward Newman. M.A.
1643	Edward Pinsent

VICARS 1660 TO 1862

1660	Henry Warren M.A.
1680	John Freke
1685	Francis Freke
1744	Thomas Freke M.A.
1777	Nicholas Thomas Freke
1824	Thomas Freke M.A.
1837	Charles Gustavus Owen B.A.
1844	Charles William Ireland Jones
1847	Harvey Marriott
1862	William Walter Edwards B.A.

VICARS 1864 TO 1994

1864	Thomas Chalk B.A.
1867	Henry Townend B.A.
1883	Frank Shewell M.A.
1887	Thomas Francis Boultbee M.A.
1907	William Hodges M.A.
1928	Herbert Francis Gane
1935	George Alfred Bliss A.K.C. H.C.F.
1955	Wilfred H.G. Summerell
1968	William S. Tyler
1977	Dr Robert J.K. Law
1994	Roderick D. Withnell

Clement Ellis, vicar of Widdecome and Loddiswell, was here in 1599, and was buried in Loddiswell. A manuscript in the Bodleian Library in Oxford states that there was a stone, within the communion rails to the memory of Clement 'Ellys'. That stone is no longer there.

Edward Pinsent lived during the Commonwealth period, and in 1650 a Parliamentary survey described him as 'Edward Pinsent an able honest man'. When he died, Henry Warren of Modbury was presented by the patron, but did not gain approval of the Commonwealth. In his place was sent Leonard Hane or Hine from Halwell. He was presented 'By the keeper of the Liberty of England, by authority of Parliament'. He had won that approval for he had been 'At arms at Oxford for Oliver Cromwell'. He married a daughter of the puritan vicar of Brent and whilst living there his daughter Mary was born. After the Restoration he was ejected and Warren was presented by the true patron in 1660, but 17 years had elapsed since he was first presented. After the death of

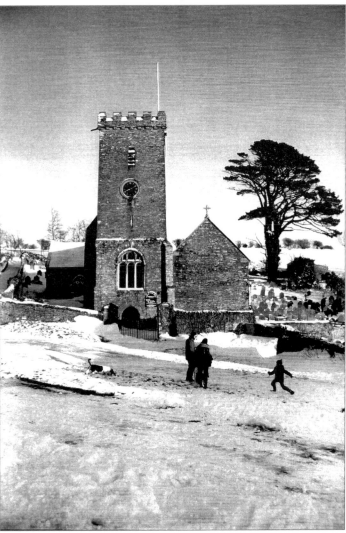

St Michael and All Angels Church, 1963.

Warren there were five vicars named Freke, followed by Gunston Owen, all of the Freke family.

In 1744 Francis Freke replied to the Bishop's queries, noting that there were 80 families in Loddiswell, 'I bless God there is no meeting house of any kind in it'. There was no public or charity school, there was an alms house but no hospital. He wrote, 'I have served the parish I hope faithfully for 55 years and upwards'. He explained that he had a large family of 12 children. Two years later his son Thomas Freke was vicar also of Little Hempstone. He mentions that now there were 'two little schools kept by two sober, religious women, where about 20 children are taught'. In 1821 Nicholas Freke said there were 158 families in Loddiswell, and that a few independents had a

meeting. He kept an assistant who lived three miles away, to whom he paid £60 a year. A pencilled note on the original document stated: 'Both Church and Chancel neglected for a long time, windows including glass tracery bad, pavement uneven – whole dirty'. Could it be that the Freke family had held the living too long? They were the patrons, so had the choice of vicar.

The patronage was let for £900 in 1633 and by 1662 it was let to Richard Freke a merchant of Exeter. In 1762 Francis Freke paid £3150 for the Rectory and tithe. The price rose each time it was sold, and in 1786 Francis Freke, having assumed the name Francis Freke Gunston, paid £5650 for the advowson (benefice). He borrowed money from William Proctor (explaining why land in the vicinity of the old Vicarage is known as Proctor's Wood).

The ecclesiastical census for 1851 can be seen in the Public Record Office in London. On the afternoon of 30 March 1851 Loddiswell had 355 people in church. There were four places of worship in the parish, and the total number worshipping in various places was 741. There was a fifth place of worship in a private house, which met only in the evening so was not counted.

In 1956 a new Rectory was built at Quarry Park and the old Vicarage, later to become Fernhill House, was sold. The Loddiswell and Woodleigh Parochial Parishes were amalgamated and the Rev. Summerell came to live in the new Rectory. In 1977 the parishes of Loddiswell and Woodleigh were further merged with Morleigh and Halwell and put in the care of Dr Robert Law.

A Team Ministry was inaugurated in 1994 when the Rev. Roderick Withnell and his family came to Loddiswell and lived in the new Vicarage at Littlegate.

41

Loddiswell Church Sunday School, 1954.
In the background: ? (vicar), Jack Hine, Reg Finnemore, Bert Bowden.
Left to right: Rodney Brooking, Johnny Marsh, Adrian Brooking, John Commons,
Rev. George Bliss, Carol Jackson, Mrs Bliss, Delia Commons, Joan Finnimore, Sandra Hine, Annette Riggall.
In front: M. Jackson, Dennis Robinson, Michael Marshall, Terry Marshall.

Mothers' Union at the Loddiswell Vicarage, c.1930.
(Left to right), back row: Eva Kernick, Blanche Tarr, Louise Hambley, Sara Guest, Louisa Hingston,
Mary Sampson, Louisa Yalland, Gladys Eastley, Emily Whittle, Florence Brown, ?;
middle row: Granny Brooking, Eva Clayton, Elizabeth Eastley, Jane Preston, Mrs Hyne, Selina Elliott,
Sarah Popplestone, Mary Jane Hodder;
front row: Ivy Luscombe, Nurse Guest, Annie Pedrick, Emma Jane Mortimore, Mrs Gane, Miss Owen,
Mrs Collins, Marion Hyne, Jenny Ryder, Ethel Eastley, Ada Hine.

✄ Sunday School ✄

During the period from the late 1970s to the arrival of the Rev. Roderick Withnell in 1994, there had not been a Sunday School. Children of the parish attended the Congregational Sunday School. However, several families with young children had joined the church for services and in the spring of 1995 a Sunday School started up with Mrs Alison Withnell leading a small group of children at the temporary Vicarage in Wyselands Barn on the second and fourth Sundays during the morning services.

As numbers grew and a permanent Vicarage was found some distance from the church, other accommodation had to be arranged. The provision of screening for the Wise Chapel, creating a new room within the church, enabled the Sunday School to take place during the services.

More recently the age range and increasing number of children attending, together with a group of additional helpers and teachers, has led to the creation of two classes. The Priest's room above the porch, which had been a store room, was beautifully renovated with voluntary help from within the church to become an ideal room in which older children could gather. The ever-growing numbers of toddlers and juniors continue to meet in the Wise Chapel Room for their Sunday School.

Loddiswell Sunday School, 1999.
Left to right: Sophie Elliott, Chloe Harvey, Sarah Hudson, Louise George (in front), Alison Withnell with Juliet and Eleanor, Karen Elliott with Edmund Withnell, Amy Elliott, Philippa Hyne, Kate Harvey, Rachel George, Anna Harvey (in front).

The Church Through the Ages

There was a Saxon church in Loddiswell in the time of Hecca the Saxon Lord, but the oldest parts of the present church were built in Norman times. The tower, nave and chancel were built c.AD1150 to 1400 and on the south side of the altar there is a small piscina for Holy water, and a sedilia or seat dating from between 1190 to 1250. Since then parts of the walls and windows have been repaired and replaced.

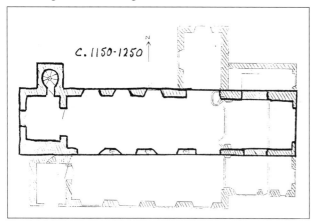

Around 1400 the north and south transepts were added making the church into a cruciform shape. At this time the north chapel was added and, in building the pillars of the church, the hagioscopes or 'squints' incorporated, which allowed those seated in the transepts to see the priest at the altar. The pillars and arches were built with flat blocks of sedimentary stone and are noticeable where the openings were made from the nave to the transepts and from the chancel to the north chapel. The small blocked archway from the north transept to the north chapel is of a similar construction, and a new arch was built between the nave and the chancel.

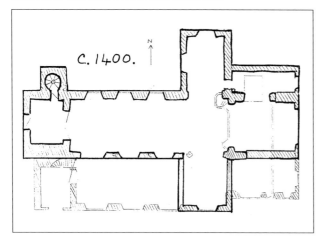

About 1430 a south chapel, now the Lady Chapel, was added. It had become a custom for south chapels to be used for penances and prayers for the 'wealthy departed' who often left funds for those who prayed for their souls, a practise which was discontinued at the Dissolution of the Monasteries. Openings had to be made from the new south chapel to the chancel and to the south transept, and arches had to be erected. Granite from Dartmoor was used for this purpose and was cut to a semi-octagonal shape.

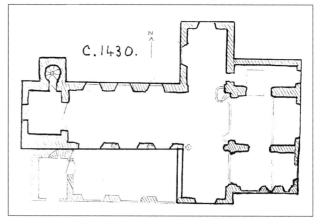

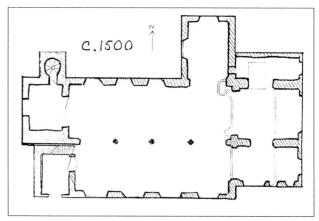

In the 15th century everyone was expected to attend at least one service on Sundays. In fact, many years later in 1581, during the reign of Queen Elizabeth I, the Recusancy Law was passed under which parishioners could be fined or imprisoned for holding or attending Mass or for not attending church. The increasing population made it necessary to enlarge the church and in about 1500 the south aisle was added. The south transept was demolished by removing the south and west walls, and the south wall of the nave was replaced by four fluted granite columns and three granite arches. The fourth stone arch was retained, being propped up with timber supports to rest one end on the new granite column.

At the south end of the church the porch was added with a priest's room above to provide a

October/November

40p

Grapevine

In this issue:
A Russian Experience
Thanksgiving in the U.S.A.

Top: The 'little flock' keeps the old churchyard tidy.
Above: Church door lock and key.
Left: Grapevine, *the Parish Magazine.*

temporary rest for the priest who had travelled some distance on horseback.

Many churches at this time were open plan with the congregation standing around in groups. Older members would 'go to the wall' where there was a plinth on which to sit. This open arrangement did not satisfy the aristocracy who had high-sided box pews built for their privacy. At Loddiswell, Sunday School scholars occupied one or two box pews and often found something to interest them through the long, boring sermon. On one occasion a clock had been dismantled and rebuilt when, in the silence of the church except

for the preacher's words, a voice piped up 'There is another little wheel here, Ned'.

Thomas Chalk became vicar in 1864 – a report in the *Kingsbridge Gazette* the following June states:

We are glad to hear that strenuous efforts are being made by the Vicar and inhabitants of this parish to restore the church with an entirely new open timber roof to the nave, and a roof to the south aisle to correspond and new seats throughout the church, and to open out the tower arch and window, doing away with the hideous galleries... in front of them.

Above: Loddiswell Church Organ built in 1866 by Mr Dicker of Exeter at a cost of £200. It was restored in 1999 at a cost of £7400.

Left: Hilary Hudson at the organ, 1998.

✄ Church Music and Organ ✄

Music in churches was discouraged by the Puritans and by 1644 most church organs had been destroyed. Singing was at that time unaccompanied until the musical life of the church was revived by the Wesleys. Local musicians were recruited to lead the choirs through hymns and psalms. Galleries were built at the west end of churches for the bands and singers. In 1818, Robert Popplestone, the carpenter, was instructed to build a gallery at the back of the church near the belfry for the band and choir. The total cost of the construction was £34.

Clergy generally found that with the musicians and choir at the back of the church they were inclined to lose control of the service. When the musicians led the hymns and psalms the congregation would rise and turn 'to face the music'. Any new arrangement would need to bring the music and choir to the front.

In 1866, the issue of equipping the church with a new organ was reported in the *Kingsbridge Gazette*:

The Vicar is anxious not only to improve the fabric of the church itself but also the worship of God in that fabric by substituting a good organ in place of the harmonium and various other instruments, which at present lead the singing.

Kingsbridge Gazette, 1 December 1866:

The fine organ built by Mr Dicker of Exeter was opened with such success as will be long remembered. As the Clergy and Choir entered, the triumphal notes of 'The Strain Upraise' burst forth both from those assembled in the Church and from the surplused procession.

The whole of the accompaniment and voluntaries were magnificently played by Mr R.E. West who fully proved the excellent character of the instrument committed to his charge. He also played compositions of a high order including 'The Wedding March' from Athalie and several others. Mr West, a Professor of Music, was a pupil of Herr Weber, organist of the Royal Chapel, Saint James' Palace, and other Masters of the Royal Academy of Music. Twelve clergymen were present and every preparation had been made for the comfort of the visitors, and lunch and tea were provided in the schoolroom at the Church House Inn. Singers from Kingsbridge, West Alvington, Modbury and Loddiswell gave a more powerful choir than has ever been heard in the neighbourhood.

The receipts from the services was £25.12s.6d. towards the cost of the organ of £200. The total cost of restoring the Church was £1500 which now has 450 sittings.

Loddiswell Church Choir, 1997.
Left to right: Rev. Roderick Withnell, Ken Hudson, Hilary Hudson,
Sir William Peek, Jean Lidstone, John Came, Jane Brooking, Mac Carter, Rosie Pritchard, Sue Wildig (front),
Eric Cooke, Lady Lucy Peek, Joan Parkes, Betty Sampson, Paul Worden.

Loddiswell Church Choir outing at Berry Pomeroy Castle, 1900.
(Left to right) back row: Mr Isaacs, F. Pope, William Hingston, Joseph Cranch, Robert Skinner,
William W. Elliott, Thomas Prouse, William Elliott, Rev. T.E. Boultbee, William Preston;
middle row: John Prouse, William Osborn, Sarah Prouse, Florence Preston, Selina Elliott, Laura Yalland,
Nellie Elliott, Mabel Waldron, Annie Hingston;
front row: Horace Preston, Reginald Luscombe, ? Waldron, Arthur Elliott, Rosie Preston, Emmie Hingston.

Loddiswell Church Choir outing to Bulleigh Barton, Totnes, 1910.
(From left to right) back row: ? Head, Philip Lakeman, Edwin Preston, Robert Skinner, John Yalland,
William Hingston, Arthur Preston;
3rd row: George Osmond, William W. Elliott, Jimmy Middlewick, William Elliott, William Preston,
John Prouse, William Osborn, Albert Preston;
2nd row: Florence Preston, Bessie Lakeman, Minnie Prouse, Selina Elliott, Carrie Hingston,
Nelly Kerswell (née Elliott), Rev. W. Hodges, ?, Joe Cranch; front row: ?.

Loddiswell Church Choir, 1960.
From left to right: Dulcie Garland, Betty Lethbridge, Phyllis Robinson, Rosemary Harding, Florrie Hine, Annette Napeon (née Riggall), Ethel Whitell, Delia Wallis (née Commons), Michael Marshall, Arthur Riggall, Roger Pope, Alan Pope, John Commons, Arthur Preston, Sidney Scoble (behind).

Rev. W. Tyler with members and friend of the Church Choir, 1970.
(Left to right) back row: Rev. Tyler, Dennis Sharland, Jim Hine, Felicity Harvey, Geraldine Wakeman, Rosemary Harding, Doris Sharland, Harold Mitchell (driver), Eva Taylor, Mrs Tyler, Sheelagh Taylor, Gladys Brooking, Dulcie Garland, Rosie Lee, Violet Quick, Phyllis Harding, Nellie Baker, Rev. Herbert Jefferson, Doris Jefferson, Peggy Riggall, Joan Brooking, Jane Preston, Phyllis Robinson, Mrs Brice; front row: Rosemary Brice, Beverley Pridham, ?, Christine Brooking, Doreen Sharland, John Hyne, Gillian Robinson, Julian Taylor, David Sharland, Roger Garland, James Baker, Francis Baker, Judith Hyne, Jackie Hyne.

From the north transept window on the west side, the shields showing the arms of Devon's hereditary earls. Top left: Raleigh of Warkleigh; top centre: Gylle impaled quarterly 194 Meynard, 243 Plessey; top right: Fortescue of Wood (reversed in window); centre right: Ferrers of Churchstow impaled (reversed in window); bottom right: Arundell (of Hatch Arundell Loddiswell) of Wardour and Lanherne; centre bottom: Yarde of Churston Ferrers; bottom left: Pawlett (or Paulett) of Hinton St George, Somerset; centre left: Courtney (Earl of Devon).

⚔ Features ⚔

WINDOWS

Many of the windows are of perpendicular design and are dated between 1390 and 1420. Those in the south aisle match the period of the building of that part of the church (i.e.1500) but the mullions are later, about 1580 to 1600.

The large window on the south side of the Lady Chapel is also perpendicular (c.1450-80) and has an interesting outside tracery of rhyolite. This is an acid, igneous rock which has the appearance of lava and is found in a South Hams quarry.

At the east end of the chancel above the altar and reredos, is an impressive Victorian stained-glass window donated by the Peek family which depicts Christ blessing the children.

The north transept has a window in the north wall which shows St Michael slaying the serpent with St Peter and St Paul on either side and, on the west side, a window containing panels of medieval armorial glass. The eight shields (*see opposite*) show the arms of the hereditary Earls of Devon and above in the top lights are four badges of the Tudors – the portcullis gate, the Tudor Rose, the fleur-de-lis and the pomegranate. The last badge was the personal emblem of Queen Catherine of Aragon, the first wife of Henry VIII. After Henry's divorce the badge was no longer used. It must, therefore, have been placed here between 1509-30, making it a rare and important piece.

Top right: The tracery of the south window of the Lady Chapel.

Above: North transept window (Wise Chapel).

Right: Fleur-de-lis and the Pomegranate, the emblem of the Queen Catherine of Aragon until 1530.

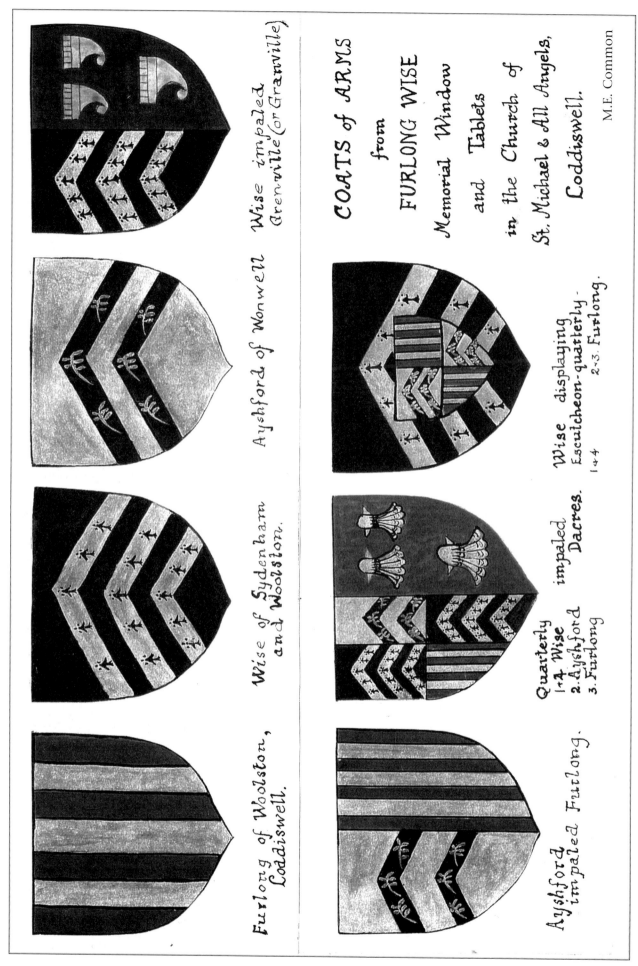

Wise impaled Grenville (or Granville)

Ayshford of Wonwell

Wise of Sydenham and Woolston.

Furlong of Woolston, Loddiswell.

COATS of ARMS
from
FURLONG WISE
Memorial Window
and Tablets
in the Church of
St. Michael & All Angels,
Loddiswell.

M.E. Common

Wise displaying Escutcheon-quarterly-
1.4.
2.3. Furlong.

impaled Dacres.

Quarterly
1.4 Wise
2. Ayshford
3. Furlong

Ayshford impaled Furlong.

The three walls of the north transept have 21 mural tablets commemorating various members of the Wise, Osmond and Furlong families. The finest is to Admiral William Furlong Wise (*see opposite*), who died in 1844. The white marble inscription tablet has a plain-pointed pediment above, containing a crest of a demi-lion. The plain lower cornice has a shield of arms and the whole is set on a black marble slab.

The oldest stone is on the north wall and commemorates Edward Furlong who died in 1616. It is inscribed: 'Fear not to dy, Learne this of me, No ill in death, If good thou be'.

A large, carved oak eagle lectern stands to the right of the chancel steps with the Victorian pulpit on the left. It commemorates Richard Peek who died in 1867 and is built against a pillar where it is entered by a flight of steps. The top is carved in alabaster, coloured red (due to iron deposits), and moulded with a narrow band of dog-tooth decoration. Below and on each side is a heavily-moulded, trefoiled arch supported on short, round columns with carved foliage capitals. The background to the arches is also of red alabaster, and the spandrels (the area outside the arches) are decorated with simple, flat flower carving. The bottom edge of each side is decorated with two flat roundels also in alabaster, and the whole structure stands on a large, squat centre pillar with four smaller columns grouped around it all on a moulded base.

Like many Devon churches, St Michael and All Angels had a chancel screen with rood loft above. Sadly this has long since vanished (possibly during the Reformation), but the pins for the door are above the pulpit by the door itself and the steps to the door are inside today's organ loft.

Above right: Eagle lectern.

Far right and right: The screen to the north transept erected in 1997; the Norman font.

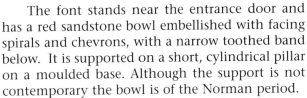

Below: The alms and deeds chest.

The font stands near the entrance door and has a red sandstone bowl embellished with facing spirals and chevrons, with a narrow toothed band below. It is supported on a short, cylindrical pillar on a moulded base. Although the support is not contemporary the bowl is of the Norman period.

The Breeches Bible was printed in London in 1583 by Queen Elizabeth's printer Christopher Barker. It is dedicated 'To The Most Vertuous and

Noble Ladie Elizabeth, Queen of England, France and Ireland' It is a 'Breeches Bible' in that it translates part of Genesis 3.7 as 'they sewed figgetree leaves together and made themselves breeches'. Later translations used the word 'aprons'. It was presented by the family of Lt Col. D.W. Wise of Alleron after his death in 1918.

The oak arms and deed chest was originally fitted with three locks with different keys, one each for the vicar and two churchwardens. None could open the chest without the agreement of the other two.

At the Reformation all churches were required to display the Royal Arms, which were presumably renewed with each new occupant of the throne. The practice, although revived intermittently, gradually fell into disuse. The arms of George III are displayed over the main doorway.

A sound-proof oak chancel screen, with the upper panels double glazed, was erected in 1997 filling the archway between the nave and the north transept (or Wise Chapel). It was constructed to provide a room for the Sunday School and for meetings of the Parochial Church Council. The chapel is well placed for use as a vestry and is considerably larger than that behind the organ.

Roof slates on the church have been regularly replaced when necessary but by 1990 it was evident that major work was needed to be undertaken. The lead gutter between the divided roofs had deteriorated and was replaced in 1991 at a cost of £7554. Five years later work began on capping the main walls with lead and replacing the gutters and down pipes. The south side was completed in 1996 at a cost of £3682 and part of the north side in 1997.

In 1987/8 linquartz heaters were installed in the nave and chancel replacing the pew tubular heaters and in 1997 the lighting and heating in the Wise Chapel were also improved.

Top: The pulpit commemorates Richard Peek who died in 1867.

Above: 'Will it go through the door?' Left to right: Douglas Tarr, Bill Penwill and Russell Baker installing the church safe in 1997.

George III coat of arms, 1819.

⚒ The Bells of Loddiswell ⚒

The first record of the bells dates from the reign of Edward VI in 1553 when it was noted 'Loddyswell 1111 belles in the tower their'. By 1865 Loddiswell had five bells, two being crazed or broken, but a few years later the Vestry Book states 'It was the wish of many of the parishioners that an additional bell should be obtained and that they might have the pleasure of hearing a good peel of 6 bells'. A Bell Committee was formed in 1877 to obtain estimates for the work. The Captain of the Ringers at that time was William Elliott, grandfather of Owen Elliott and Betty Sampson. The work was undertaken by John Taylor & Co., The Bell Foundry, Loughborough, who recast the then 3rd and tenor bells which were cracked, and added a new treble to make the present ring of six bells.

In 1910 steel joists and a cast-iron frame were put in place and the bells re-hung by Mr Aggett of Chagford. The 4th bell was mounted direct onto the steel joists placed above the other five bells which were hung in a bellframe of cast-iron sections secured to the floor of the bellchamber.

In 1967 Loddiswell craftsmen Russell Baker and Basil Taylor added support by building in two more steel girders and some wooden beams. In 1969 the bells were re-hung on ball-bearings making then easier to swing. There are 385 rings of bells in Devon, compared with Scotland's 15 rings, Ireland's 35 (15 of which are in N. Ireland), America's 19, Canada's 8 and South Africa's 6.

The Tapp Memorial Six Bell Festival has been held at St Michael and All Angels Church, Loddiswell since 1968. It is an annual competition for a Perpetual Silver Cup presented by Mr Ruben Tapp of Chevithorne. Another cup was purchased by the Ringers in 1992 in memory of their long-time Captain, Fred Parsliffe, and this is presented to the runners-up in the competition. Many teams of bellringers compete and then share an excellent tea provided for them in the Village Hall by the wives and families of the Loddiswell Ringers. The Loddiswell team travels to many other churches in Devon to compete in their various competitions.

No. 1	Treble added by John Taylor & Co.	1877	wt.4.25 cwt.	dia. 2' 2"
No. 2	Cast by John & Christopher Pennington of Lezant & Stoke Climsland. Embossed J[ ]P C[ ]P, i.e. John & Christopher Pennington.	1782	4.75	2'4"
No. 3	Cast by Pennington & recast by J. Warner, London (business closed). Embossed 'In Memoriam Edward VII REGIS VALCI PACIFICI ET PACIFICATORIS'. Translated In Memory of Edward VII 'a ring singularly peaceful & peacemaking'	1910	5.25	2'5"
No. 4	Cast by Pennington 1782. Recast by John Taylor & Co.	1782 1877	6.25	2'7.5"
No. 5	Cast by Pennington, inscribed 'Nicholas Luscombe & William Pitts'.	1790	6.25	2'9"
No. 6	Cast by Pennington. Originally inscribed Nicks Freke, Vicar. Edward Hellier & Thomas Willing, Churchwardens. Recast by John Taylor & Co. Embossed 'IHS' which means 'Jesus, Saviour of Men'.	1782 1877	9.5	3' 2.5"

Above: The Loddiswell Ringers, 1952.
Left to right: Bill Freeman, Arthur Preston, Glyn Brooking, Fred Parsliffe, Fred Kernick, William Taylor.

Left and right: Two of the parish's younger bellringers, Basil Taylor and Edwin Lethbridge, ringing in 1962.

Right: In 1999 the Loddiswell Ringers were successful in winning the Deanery Competition.

Previous page: Loddiswell Ringers, 1999. Left to right: Harry Bardens (capt.), Russell Baker, John Came, Edwin Lethbridge, Roy Hockin, Terry Hockin, Stephen Freeman, Cyril Freeman, Francis Baker.

Woodleigh Deanery Bell Ringers Association
ANNUAL FESTIVAL
LODDISWELL - 1st MAY 1999

PRESIDENT
E. PUNCHARD

Hon. Secretary
J. Rhymes

Judges
Mrs. P. JOHNSTONE
J. DARKE
S. ADAMS

TEAM

Treble	H. BARDENS (Cap)
2nd	E. LETHBRIDGE
3rd	C. FREEMAN
4th	J. CAME
5th	S. FREEMAN
Tenor	T. HOCKIN

Priest in Charge
Rev. R. D. WITHNELL

SHIELD & 1st CERTIFICATE
SENIOR SECTION
Awarded to *LODDISWELL*

The original set of 25 handbells was bought by the church in 1920. They were used quite often by residents of Loddiswell Parish and during the Second World War they were rung by the Youth Club. After this period a small team got together to ring the bells mainly at Christmas, but occasionally around the village and at weddings when requested.

In the early 1970s the W.I. decided they would like to form a team, and indeed many turned up for the first few weeks. Gradually the numbers decreased but led by Mr Kenneth Hyne the following team was formed: Janet Beckley, Muriel Carpenter, Angela Freeman, Ruth Hyne, Hazel Lethbridge and Sylvia Walke. Practice night was in the Village Hall and when that was not available the team used the Chapel Hall, eventually moving to the home of Ken and Ruth Hyne where they have now been practising for many years. The team is now the Loddiswell Handbell Ringers rather than the Loddiswell W.I. Handbell Ringers so that members outside the W.I. can be included.

After raising enough money the ringers sent the bells to the Whitechapel Bell Foundry, London (where they were originally cast), for re-furbishing and to add extra bells to the set. The overhauled bells looked and sounded wonderful. Some of the new bells were donated by families of the ringers and one by the W.I.

The team joined the Association of Handbell Ringers of Great Britain and have enjoyed the friendship of teams throughout the country ever since. The team has travelled across the country; to Sheffield University, Lancaster, Guildford, Reading, Wolverhampton, Lowestoft, Swansea and Exeter. When visiting Lancaster the team arrived at the University and checked in to the allocated rooms surrounding a beautiful quadrangle, in the middle of which stood a huge tree. It was covered in pink blossom and everyone was keen to take some photographs. On taking a closer look one could see that the tree was covered in pink toilet tissue which proved to be the joke of the weekend. When attending these rallies the team learned a great deal which they have since put into practice.

An Annual Rally is held on the first Saturday in May when Loddiswell invite other teams from the South West to take part. This is greatly enjoyed by everyone who attends.

Each year the team ring for many good causes and raise substantial amounts for charity. Outdoor ringing is not ideal for handbells as, having to contend with wind, the sound does not carry as well as indoors. Recently the team purchased eight more handbells. They are secondhand and in need of considerable renovation, but craftsman, Mr Geoff Hill of Lamerton, has agreed to carry out the work.

Above: The Loddiswell Handbell Ringers, 1998.
(Left to right) back row: Angela Freeman, Sally Dutton, Ken Hyne, Janet Beckley, Catherine Taylor,
Sylvia Walke; front row: Muriel Carpenter, Sylvia Hallam, Eileen Gray, Hazel Lethbridge, Ruth Hyne.
Six of the original team, started in the early 1970s, are still ringing today.

Easter bazaar helpers and friends outside the Congregational Hall, 1938.
(Left to right) standing: Ivy Hine, Mabel Gerry, Mrs Butters, Rev. R. Maliphant (at rear), Mrs Maliphant,
Annie Hine, Rex Gerry, Will Harding, Phyllis Jeffery, Mary Ann Harding, Emma Hine, Len Scobell,
Mary Harding, Eva Taylor, Nell Scobell, Tom Brooking, Majorie Brooking;
front row: Ethel Eva Hine, Stewart Gerry, Eveline Hine, Ethel Hine, Joan Taylor, Mrs Peter Hine, Stella Hine,
Amber Ryder, Phyllis Elliott, Gwendoline Hine, Alice Taylor.

Congregational Church Sunday School, 1964.
(Left to right) back row: Colin Harvey, Linda Edgcombe, Jennifer Edgcombe, Rosemary Martin,
Heather Harding, Susan Martin;
3rd row: Peter Jeffery, Michael Jeffery, Reeta Hine, ?, Andrew Edgcombe, Felicity Harvey, Rosemary Harding,
Ethel Hine, Sydney Jeffery;
2nd row: Trevor Harvey, Pauline Ryder, Helen Martin, Paul Jeffery;
front row: Christopher Lloyd, Phillip Martin, Elizabeth Hine, Jonathan Lloyd, Keith Martin, Nigel Harvey,
Lorna Jeffery, Heather Martin, John Jeffery (in front).

Chapter 8: The Congregational Church

The first Congregational Church in Loddiswell was opened in 1808. Known as the Providence Independent Chapel, it was situated in the Congregational graveyard, where the shelter now stands. There were Congregationalists (or Independents as they were then called) worshipping in Loddiswell at even an earlier date. It was customary for early dissenters to hold their meetings in private dwelling houses, as did Rev. John Flavel in Dartmouth in the 17th century. Another such instance can be quoted from the ecclesiastical census of 1851, for in that year a Methodist congregation met in Loddiswell in the house of Mr William Willing. The first Independents in Loddiswell must have started with a nucleus of people worshipping in a private house or wherever convenient, until such time as the way was made clear for them to build their first chapel.

Mr Bob Nunn, aged 91, at the organ for the 100th Anniversary Service in 1964.

One cannot embark upon the history of this church without some mention of the early story of the Protestant religion in the parish. During the Civil War, when England was being torn asunder by variance of opinion, there was in Loddiswell a vicar who was acceptable to the Cromwellian Puritans. As previously mentioned, a Parliamentary Survey in 1650 describes that vicar as one 'Edward Pinsent an able honest man Incumbent there receiveth the profits of the Vicarage'. Pinsent remained vicar until his death in 1652, when Henry Warren of Modbury was presented. He was not accepted and could get no institution. Instead of Warren, the licence to be Loddiswell's vicar was given to Leonard Hayne (who was 'At arms at Oxford for Oliver Cromwell').
. After the Restoration he was ejected from Loddiswell and went to South Tawton but did not conform. The next we hear of him was after St Bartholomew's Day 1662 when greater freedom was given to the ministers. Some 22 ejected ministers came to live in Exeter and amongst them on the list is 'Leonard Hyne, formerly of Loddiswell'. Later he was living on his own property at West Alvington.

In 1673 Arthur Langworthy of Hatch Arundell, Loddiswell, gave a piece of land at Venn to the Baptists of Kingsbridge for the quiet burial of those who had passed away 'in these troublous times'. 'Troublous' they certainly were: Kingsbridge had become the home of several ejected ministers; John Hicks, George Hughes, Jellinger and Quick. Two others, Tooker and Burdwood, lived within the area. They preached wherever they could with reasonable safety. John Hicks preached secretly at Surley Butts, or Sorley Green as it is now named, and on the Saltstone in the Estuary. People who came from the surrounding villages held their religion dear and were willing to risk persecution for their religious freedom.

The Conventicle Act of 1670 made it illegal to hold an assembly of five persons or more in addition to those of the household for religious purposes. The punishments for breaching this were:

1. Both preacher and owner of house to be fined £20.
2. Poor people 5/- for first offence, double for second offence. This fine could be levied on any 'well to do person' up to £10, if the poor could not pay.
3. Fines collected were given one third to the Poor Fund, one third to Treasury, and one third to informer(s).

These fines were severe when wages were ls.4d. a day and cottage rents £2.10s. a year so it is not surprising that informers in the South Hams were well known to the Nonconformists.

It is an interesting fact that the most persecuted man in Exeter was a fuller named Thomas Crispin. Born in Kingsbridge, he founded the Kingsbridge Grammar School and also owned land in Loddiswell. In 1673 he shared the minister's fine in John Palmer's house, the minister being John Hicks. Crispin (or Crispyne) was fined regularly for holding meetings in his own house in Exeter – for example, a £20 fine in 1675 and 1676 and another fine in 1677 when three persons were assembled in his home.

A document dated 1670 comes a little nearer to Loddiswell. Arthur Langworthy held a meeting in his house at Churchstow with more than 50 people present. The informers were able to catch and name 12 people, one of whom was Richard West of Loddiswell. They were fined 5 shillings each and Arthur Langworthy had to pay £20.

Loddiswell was surrounded by people with strong Puritan sympathies. Sir Edmund Fowell of Fowelscombe was one such, as also were the Langworthys of Hatch Arundell. Mistress Gertrude Langworthy owed five weeks' martial rate (6 shillings) and refused to pay. It must be remembered that the great Parliamentarian, Sir John Eliot, was a kinsman of the Langworthy family and Eliot had been imprisoned for his Parliamentarian activities, dying in the Tower in 1632. It is not surprising that the Eliots and Langworthys leaned towards dissent and that Loddiswell, being so closely allied with earnest and influential people, was home to considerable Nonconformist following. The Compton census (1676) gives these figures for Loddiswell; 360 Conformists. No Papists. 18 Nonconformists'.

All this is a far cry from Loddiswell Congregational Church, but it does prove that the seed of the Free Church was firmly established in the parish 300 years ago. Nonconformists were encouraged when, on 8 February 1749, George Whitefield preached to 1000 people on Kingsbridge Quay. He returned on 15 February 1759 and Nathaniel Cranch of Mill Street lent him his kitchen table, now in the Congregational Church.

In the Bishop's queries for 1744 and 1746 it is stated that there was no meeting house of any kind in Loddiswell. In order to examine the need for an Independent Church one must consult the baptismal registers of both Baptist and Ebenezer (Independent or Congregational) Churches at Kingsbridge. From 1790 the names of Loddiswell and Woodleigh families appear. The Baptist register records names from Woodleigh, Goss, Partridge, Bond and Steer. From Loddiswell the children William and Elizabeth Kennard are listed as being baptised in 1794 and 1796. In Loddiswell Congregational Yard there is a memorial to William and Elizabeth Kennard in a place of honour on the old chapel wall – the Kennards must have joined Loddiswell Congregational Church. Their son, William, baptised in Kingsbridge as recorded in the Baptist register, was buried in Loddiswell yard.

There is one particularly well-known family mentioned in the Kingsbridge Ebenezer (Congregational) records. On 21 September 1800 four children of John and Susannah Peek were baptised: William (born November 1791), Mary (born 1794), Thomas (born March 1799) and James (born June 1800), all being baptised on the same day. The youngest, James, gave the land for the building of the present Congregational Church. Older children of the Peek family had been baptised in Loddiswell Parish Church. One of these was Richard Peek, who was instrumental in making today's Congregational Church a reality.

The time had come for an Independent Church to be built in

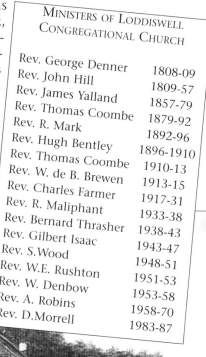

MINISTERS OF LODDISWELL CONGREGATIONAL CHURCH	
Rev. George Denner	1808-09
Rev. John Hill	1809-57
Rev. James Yalland	1857-79
Rev. Thomas Coombe	1879-92
Rev. R. Mark	1892-96
Rev. Hugh Bentley	1896-1910
Rev. Thomas Coombe	1910-13
Rev. W. de B. Brewen	1913-15
Rev. Charles Farmer	1917-31
Rev. R. Maliphant	1933-38
Rev. Bernard Thrasher	1938-43
Rev. Gilbert Isaac	1943-47
Rev. S. Wood	1948-51
Rev. W.E. Rushton	1951-53
Rev. W. Denbow	1953-58
Rev. A. Robins	1958-70
Rev. D. Morrell	1983-87

Hazelwood Chapel, one of the chapels built by Richard Peek in 1845.

Loddiswell, and it was the Rev. George Denner who undertook this onerous task. At Kingsbridge from 1803, his name appears in both the Ford baptismal register in 1804 and the Loddiswell Independent Register in August 1806 when he baptised three children, two months before coming to Loddiswell as the first minister.

Rev. Denner worked assiduously in Loddiswell on the raising of the first chapel. On 19 April 1808 the first Independent chapel was opened and was known as Providence Chapel. Rev. Denner saw his church opened, but he died just a year later at the age of 43. His memorial still stands within the walls of the remains of Providence Chapel in the Congregational Yard.

The Peek family interest actually goes back to the first chapel at the time of which their mother's family, the Foxworthys were among the early Independents of the Providence Chapel. There is a memorial to their mother's brother, John Foxworthy, aged 49, within the wall of the old Providence Chapel, and also one to his wife at a later date. John Foxworthy died and was buried in the Loddiswell Providence Yard only one year after the early chapel was built.

The second minister was Rev. John Hill and the *Congregational Year Book* in 1858 reads:

Hill, John. Loddiswell, born in Ashburton 29th May 1778; was trained to the woollen business and was promoted foreman in a large woollen factory. In the year 1801 he was visited with severe personal affliction, which, under the Divine Blessing, was the means of his conversion. When health was restored he was anxious to make 'Known to sinners around, what a dear Saviour he found'.

Right: Old Congregational Chapel, erected in 1808.

Below: George Hine taking children on their outing by the Kings Arms (Ebb Tide), Aveton Gifford, 1913.

He soon commenced preaching in various towns and villages the full, free and complete salvation for all who felt in need of a Saviour. In the year 1809 he received a unanimous call from the Independent Church at Loddiswell to become their pastor. In addition to his ministry he carried on a small woollen business until the time of his death, on 30 April 1857.

John Hill is listed in the 1841 census as a 'Woolcomber' and in the 1851 census as an Independent Minister, aged 72. At that time he had an unmarried son John (40) who was also a woolcomber and two daughters, Ann (38), and Jemima (36). Ann was a dressmaker and all of them were born in Totnes. According to the 1839 Tithe Map, it appears that the Rev. John Hill lived in Town's Lane in Vine House. Memorials of the Hill family can be seen in the graveyard.

These two ministers, George Denner and John Hill, firmly established the Providence Independent Church in Loddiswell. In order to get some idea of the spiritual and physical size of Providence Chapel, one must consult the Ecclesiastical census for 1851. There were five churches in the parish; Hazelwood Bible Christian, The Parish Church, Providence Independent, Stanton Bible Christian and the Wesleyan Methodist Preaching Room. This last place of

worship was opened in 1850 and held services on Sunday evenings. It was situated in or near Little Reads with Mr William Willing as Steward.

Providence Independent (Congregational) had provision for 180 'free sittings' and 120 'other'. Apparently it could accommodate 300 people. The congregations attending Providence Chapel on 30 March 1851 were: 'Morning 90 and 78 Sunday School, Afternoons 183 and 78 Sunday School, Evenings 187'. One notes that in the parish as a whole 741 people attended a place of worship that day. Attendances were: Hazelwood 85, Parish Church 255, Providence 261 (including Sunday School), Stanton 40. In total, the population of Loddiswell was 949 but perhaps not all of these people were from Loddiswell – it is known that Congregationalists came from a wide area and possibly some Loddiswell people may have gone out of the parish to worship.

The census mentions James Popplestone of Loddiswell who was 'minister' of Aveton Gifford Independent Church. This may have been another of the Peek family's efforts to establish another congregation in the South Hams, as at this time there was no Independent building in Aveton Gifford.

From 1830 there were baptisms of families from Halwell, Harberton, Aveton Gifford, Totnes, Modbury, Plympton, North Huish, Morleigh, Ringmore, Torquay, Woodleigh and from the length and breadth of Loddiswell Parish. These were not all just isolated cases of children being brought from other parishes. From 1830 onwards, a number of families came from Harberton, their names being Colton, Cuming, Morgan, Treby, Goodman, Sherman and Quick.

After the death of Rev. John Hill in 1857, Loddiswell had to look for another minister and found him in their midst. For a while one of the deacons, Mr James Yalland of Weeke, led the congregation. After several months it was unanimously decided to invite him to be the pastor. The minutes state 'That after having sat under Mr Yalland's ministry for many months, they have the highest opinion of his integrity and piety'.

The 1851 census gives details of James Yalland and his family. He was then 49 years of age and farmed 75 acres at Weeke. He was born in South Brent, but his wife Jane, who was 50, and twin children James and Jane, aged 16, were born in Loddiswell.

James Yalland the farmer must have done

much soul searching before accepting the ministry. However, the appointment was conditional. It was agreed that he was at liberty to resign at any time and that the church would have the same freedom. The way was made clear for him, his children were now 23 years of age.

He appears to have left Weeke, for in the 1861 census he is listed as living at the Mill Cottage. In 1867 he moved into the heart of the village and rented Pitt House and orchard at £8.10s. per annum. The House was on the site of Pitt Court,

Rev. Hugh Bentley outside his home at No.2 The Terrace.

and was one of the premises given by the Peek Family to the Chapel Trust. Here Mr Yalland saw a period of tremendous activity. He and the Independent Church received great support from the Peek Family, and particularly Richard Peek who had retired in the mid 1830s and had furthered education by providing a reading room in the village. In 1853 he gave Loddiswell a fine new school, the British School (Independent). This was a great boon to the parish for it not only provided an education for children but was also a centre for lectures, chapel teas and other social activities.

The time had come for further developments in the church for the old Providence Chapel was showing signs of decay. On Sunday 14 April 1861 it was announced from the pulpit that there would be a special church meeting to consider 'the propriety of building a new chapel near the old one'. On 26 April a building committee was formed, including: Rev. James Yalland, R. Peek Esq. (Secretary), Mr Benjamin Balkwill (Treasurer), Mr Man, Mr Richard Harvey, Mr John Popplestone, Mr C. Willing and Mr Gay.

On 14 May it was reported that James Peek Esq., of London had kindly offered to give a new site of land near the British School on which to build an Independent Chapel instead of building in the cemetery.

On Whit Monday, 25 May 1863 at 3pm the foundation stone was laid by Richard Peek Esq. The weather was good and although it was the day of the village fair and also the annual meeting and dinner of a large club held in the Church House Inn, there was a large gathering of people from Loddiswell, Kingsbridge and surrounding villages, hamlets and farms. The foundation stone reputed to be half a ton in weight had beneath it a sealed bottle containing parchment documents recording the purpose of the building, the date and names of the minister, trustees and architect. The address was given by the President of Western College from an improvised pulpit made from a pile of stones. Between 120 and 130 people sat down to tea in the British Schoolroom (today's Primary School).

The annual Sunday School treat took place in July of that year, as usual at Hazelwood, the home of Richard Peek. This treat was advertised in advance in the press, Sunday School children and their teachers were to be given their tea, other persons were to pay 1 shilling each. The whole proceeds were to be given to the building of the new chapel at Loddiswell. 'Ladies and Gentlemen' were 'respectfully invited to be present' and it was an ideal day – Sunday School children came from Loddiswell, Aveton Gifford, Stanton, Morleigh, Ugborough and Brent, with visitors arriving from all directions; Salcombe, Stokenham, Brent Ugborough, Modbury and from farms and hamlets between. They were given the freedom of Hazelwood House and grounds and the children were given their tea on the green, after which the adults sat down in a gaily-decorated loft to their own feast, 400 of them paying their 1 shilling for the privilege and no doubt many more subscribing further towards the new chapel.

The opening of the new Congregational Church at Loddiswell took place in October 1864 amid great rejoicing. The building is said to have cost £870 which included the boundary walls, gates and railings – it has been kept an active, live Church by its faithful Church members ever since.

James Peek is also remembered for founding the Peek Prize Scripture Scheme. This scheme is open to all schools in Plymouth and the South Devon area, and many bibles, books and certificates have been won by Loddiswell children through the years.

Laurel Cottage was purchased in 1920 for a manse and sold again in 1956 after a new manse was built on land at the top of the burial ground near Village Cross road.

Worshippers used to tether their horses in stables close to the church. When these fell into a dangerous state they were demolished and Mr. F. J. Harvey of Higher Grimpstonleigh acquired the land and gave it to the church for a hall to be built with stables underneath. These were later made into garages. The hall was opened on 17 July 1930 and has been greatly used ever since for meetings and numerous social and fund-raising events. In the 1940s and '50s, special Easter bazaars were held here, always with a particular theme. Special objects were made in which to place the Easter gift envelopes, including a pie, bird's nest, crown, fishpond and a model of the church, and there was an evening concert to finish off the day. Various children's meetings have been held over the years, including Junior Christian Endeavour, Sunshine Corner, Crusaders, Young People's Fellowship and Sunday School. Ship halfpennies were collected and brought by the children to help fund the John Williams Missionary Ships and other missionary funds were also raised by children and supervised by adults, who picked primroses in Back Lane (Ham Butts to Mill Hill), tying up 40 buds and a trio of leaves with a piece of wool.

In 1982 the Sunday School needed extra classrooms and the three garages underneath the main hall were converted into rooms. These are now regularly used by the Women's Guild, Parish Council and various other organisations.

When the Congregational Church in Kingsbridge was bombed in January 1943, the splendid pipe organ was salvaged and given to the Loddiswell Congregational Church. It was dedicated by the Rev. G. Isaac (pastor) in June 1946 at a special service when the organ was unveiled by Mrs Viles of Kingsbridge. The Rev. V. Tudor of

Above: West end of the Congregational Chapel built in 1863 by Richard Peek of Hazelwood.

Left: Painting by the Rev. Hugh Bentley in 1899 of the east end of the Congregational Church from the New Road.

Torquay was the preacher and Mr J.R. Nunn presided at the organ. Mr Nunn was organist at the Kingsbridge church from 1926 until it was bombed in 1943. From 1954 to 1967 he came to Loddiswell almost every Sunday to play for the Evening Service, and often travelled to Sorley Green by the Totnes bus, covering the remainder of his journey on foot. Quite frequently he walked all the way from Kingsbridge during the afternoon although he was over 80.

A group was formed between Loddiswell, Torcross, Dartmouth and Stokefleming Congregational Churches in 1970 and the manse at Loddiswell was sold. A joint manse was bought in Dartmouth with the intention of having a minister to serve all four churches. In 1972 each Congregational and Presbyterian Church was asked to vote on a union to form the United Reformed Church. Loddiswell and Torcross did not wish to join this union and voted against it so the manse in Dartmouth was once again sold.

To commemorate the tercentenary of the Ejectment of 1662, a special service was arranged in 1962 at one of the original sites at Sorley Green. The moderator, Rev. Charles Haig, conducted this service as well as the Loddiswell Congregational Centenary Service two years later in 1964.

In the early 1970s four young people formed a music group and produced several concerts as well as playing in the church. Another music group has recently been formed and plays on special occasions. Since 1972 the church has been affiliated to the Congregational Federation whose headquarters are in Nottingham and we were privileged to make the banner for the South West Area which was displayed at the 25th anniversary celebrations in Nottingham on 11 October 1997. The church joined Kingsbridge District Churches Together in 1986 and has been actively involved ever since.

The Church roof was badly damaged in gales during the early months of 1987 and was replaced with a new roof the following Autumn. £10 000 was needed, a daunting prospect for a small church, and a special appeal was made. Many fund-raising events were organised by members and numerous donations were given enabling the roof to be paid for in less than a year – a remarkable effort. The church was completely re-decorated in the Autumn of 1996 following extensive work to replace the cornices on both sides which had become unsafe.

Richard Peek

Richard Peek was born in Loddiswell in 1782. He moved to Kingsbridge, and later to Plymouth where he worked in a grocer's business and gained experience in commerce. In 1807 he left Plymouth and walked to London to seek employment. He chanced to meet a Quaker in London whom he had seen before in Kingsbridge. He explained his need for employment and the Quaker, obviously recognising honesty and integrity, recommended him to a tea broker.

He took his place in the warehouse of Sanderson & Barclay where he worked for seven years, after which he received promotion and was elevated to the position of traveller, his brother, William, taking his place in the warehouse. Their younger brother James (12), came up to London and joined them where he received his education and training under his siblings' careful watch.

After a while it became apparent that the Peek brothers had a flair for business and they were determined to branch out on their own. They saw that the system of trading could be improved and decided that if grocers were willing to settle their accounts within a month of delivery, they could supply them with tea at a cheaper rate.

William was the first to set up the business. Grocers were not slow to take advantage of this business proposition. A London Directory mentions William Peek, tea merchant in 1818. Richard and James followed into the business and by 1923 Peek Bros & Co. were firmly settled in business in Coleman Street where they prospered and expanded.

When the East India Company's tea and coffee monopoly was abolished in Liverpool, Peek branches were set up there. Later, the Liverpool branches traded under the name of Peek Bros & Winch. It is interesting to hear from Mr John Brooke of Brooke Bond Liebig Co, that the founder of the Brooke Bond Tea Company was taken as a pupil in the Peek's Liverpool branch in 1865 and later transferred to the London branch.

Richard Peek was a great exponent of anti slavery and his portrait has been in the National Portrait Gallery with a group of men all of whom advocated anti slavery.

In 1829 he became a member of the Corporation of London and in 1832, Sheriff of London. Soon after he retired to Hazelwood where he devoted his time to magisterial duties and to philanthropic activities. From then on James and William shouldered the responsibility of the tea business.

In 1857 James Peek branched into biscuits making, bringing into the business a Mr George Hender Frean who was married to his niece. The Freans were millers from Plymouth and eventually the name Peek Frean was used.

Congregational Sunday School, Women's Guild and Parish Magazine

The Sunday School was affiliated to the National Sunday School Union (later the National Christian Education Council) through the Plymouth and District Sunday School Union in November 1949. Soon afterwards, scholars commenced taking the Scripture Examination. Successful scholars were awarded Certificates and for five consecutive years a Special Certificate. The examination was set on a particular subject with passages to be studied and some memorised. On three occasions, in 1955, 1964 and 1965, the shield awarded by the Plymouth and District Sunday School Union was won by Loddiswell for gaining the most marks in the examination. Sydney Jeffery was the Superintendent of the Sunday School for 47 years from 1945 to 1992.

The Women's Guild began in 1934 for mothers and babies and soon became open to all ladies who gathered at monthly meetings with a variety of speakers. Babies were entered in the Cradle Roll and, as they became old enough, progressed to the Sunday School. For many years a summer garden meeting was held at Chevithorne and later in other members' gardens. Annual Guild services are held, often with contributions from members. In 1998 the Guild began sponsoring the education of a child from Bethany near Jerusalem as a project. Members continue to meet monthly and welcome any ladies from the village and district.

For many years Anglican Church news and information was circulated through the *Woodleigh Deanery Magazine* reporting events from all the churches. By 1974 the revenue from advertising did not cover a sufficient part of the increasing cost of printing and subscription rates were raised. It was then that Loddiswell and Woodleigh decided to pull out and discussions with other churches led to the joint production of a more local magazine for the Loddiswell Anglican and Congregational, the Woodleigh Anglican and the Torcross Congregational Churches. When a Team Ministry was established in 1994, East Allington Church joined in. The magazine was edited by Doris Jefferson in the 1970s and '80s, then by Ann Hodge and, more recently, by Irene Hulse, Frank Prowse, Eunice Yabsley and Penny Hooper.

A major contributor through the 1970s and '80s was Christian Michell who wrote about local history and events. The Magazine was renamed *The Open Door* in April 1995 and changed to *Grapevine* the following year. In addition to church and chapel news, articles are presented by parishioners who relate their experiences and write on a variety of topics.

Women's Guild outside the Congregational Hall, 1998.
(Left to right) standing: May Ryder, Jane Taylor, Olive Ellis, Hilary Field, Eileen Randall, Doreen Jarvis, Hilda Harvey, Susan Freeman, Edna Lloyd, Eunice Bidgood, Betty Thorns, Peggy Riggall, Rene Marshall, Jean Hallam, Muriel Carpenter, Jean Wood, Sylvia Hallam, Sue Ryder;
front row: Dorothy Brooking, Winnie Jeffery, De Pope, Audrey Pope, Irene Hulse, Eveline Hine.

Blackdown Rings

Above: Basil Taylor levelling the directional granite slab.

Right: Brian Widger pushing the Staddon grit stone into place for the commemorative plaque.

Above right: Donald Pethybridge and Russell Baker cleaning the stone.

Above: Rodney Swarbrick unveiling the plaque attended by Majorie Tomlinson, Devon County Councillor and Captain W.G. Peek, 10 June 1991.

Right: A staggering 1000 people chose the Rings as the place to await the total eclipse of the sun on 11 August, 1999.

Chapter 9: Blackdown Rings, Wigford Mine and Yellow Ochre

The hill fort at Blackdown Rings near Loddiswell stands in 13 acres of land and is defended by a massive earth and stone rampart with a deep outer ditch.

It was probably built soon after 400BC when there seems to have been a marked deterioration of climate with increased rainfall over Dartmoor resulting in the moor people trying to migrate to the lowlands. Blackdown is one of the best preserved of the Dartmoor Iron Age hill forts, designed to guard against attack from the moor. It lies just east of the great ridgeway from the moor to the sea.

Aerial view of the Blackdown Rings, 1985.

Well over 1000 years later the Normans took advantage of the hilltop position and built a motte and bailey in the north-west corner. Although the particular circumstances of its construction are unknown, it is likely to have been built following the conquest of Devon by William I in 1068 and the counter-attack the next year by the Ireland-based sons of Harold Godwinson (who probably landed at the mouth of the river Avon or in Salcombe harbour). Their arrival may account for the nine manors south of Loddiswell, described in the Domesday Book as 'being laid waste by Irishmen'.

The Blackdown Hill is recorded in 1546 as 'Blackdoune' and in 1752 William Chapple visited the site and drew a plan of 'The Rings' in his scrapbook. Woolcome in 1827 recorded his survey of the hill-fort and described the earthworks as being in 'a state of considerable perfection'.

This was probably because of the thorns and bracken that had overgrown the ramparts and ditches. Furze for fuel was traditionally gathered on Blackdown and the land was enclosed during the 19th century. The parishioners protested and a Commission was set up in 1854 to examine the right to cut furze on ten acres there. The Blackdown was owned by the Woolston estate when William Elliott (born 1857) worked as a youth at Woolston Farm and was often sent to Blackdown to cut and collect furze.

In 1934 the Peeks of Hazelwood bought the land from Woolston Estate and in 1988 the Peek family gave the 'Rings' to the Arundell Charity.

During 1990 the feoffees applied to Devon County Council for an Environmental Land Management Scheme Grant with the intention of clearing the scrub and opening the Rings to the public. Ten acres of the thirteen-acre site were good grassland and were grazed with sheep but the motte and bailey were overgrown with scrub, brambles and bracken.

The next 18 months were spent in clearing these areas, mainly by a contractor, and a builder was employed to repair and, where necessary, rebuild the roadside wall. A stock-proof fence was erected around the whole property, a car park cleared and hardcored and a bank formed around the perimeter. To commemorate the gift of the land to the Arundell Charity a Blackdown Stone of Staddon Grit was collected and bulldozed into place and a commemoration plaque fixed to it.

The views from the Blackdown Rings are spectacular and it was decided that a directional plaque should be put on the highest point. The stonemason chose a slab of granite from Merrivale Quarry on Dartmoor, polished and engraved it and mounted it on a pillar at the top of the motte. Information plaques were made to depict the entrance into the Iron-Age fort and on the inner bailey to show the probable view of the Norman Castle. A new survey by the Royal Commission on the Historical Monuments of England was carried out on the Rings by Robert Wilson-North and Christopher Dunn and a document produced by Devon Archaeological Society.

The official opening took place in pleasant weather on 10 June 1991. Rodney Swarbrick, President of the Country Landowners Association was the guest of honour and many other County and National dignitaries came. A fortnight later John Gummer, Minister of Agriculture who was visiting Devon, asked to visit the Rings to see for himself how, with the help of an ELMS grant, a place of historic interest could be enhanced and made accessible to the public.

Blackdown or Wigford Mine

In the Parish Church Register there is a note that in 1819 William Aaron was baptised, son of William and Elizabeth Bennet, miner, and in 1823 one Samuel Sampson was baptised, son of John and Agnes Sampson, miner. Both these fathers married Loddiswell girls and in the Marriage Records are listed as Sojourners, so obviously came from outside the parish.

It was about this time (c.1819) that a small mine was opened to find lead and copper and was about a quarter of a mile south-east of the Blackdown Rings. Thomas King in his will of 1832 granted 'Also to my wife, Mary King (Greystones) all my Right and Interest in the mine at Blackdown'. (Mary Pearce who later lived at Cross House said her mother was a Miss King and related to Thomas King.). A report of the early 1830s states:

While working a recently opened mine, copper having been the object of the search, there has been discovered a large and regular lode of silver and gold in the Wigford mine which is situated not far from Loddiswell. The ore is of a dark-grey colour, approaching to black, with a metallic lustre and upon analysis is found to consist of iron, *antimony copper, silver and gold. The lode is of considerable width and the accompanying minerals are white fluor spar, spatose iron ore, and carbonate of lime.*

New Barn was built to store and crush the copper-ore, but to do this power was needed. A long lake was made in the narrow part of an adjoining field by sealing the banks with clay so that water could be collected from the springs nearby. It would take four days for the lake to fill and this was sufficient to drive the water wheel for one day to operate the mechanical hammers crushing the ore.

A Stationery Office publication in 1956 entitled *Metalliferous Mining Region S.W. of England* states:

Loddiswell Mine. The remains of the engine house and dumps of this mine are 450 yards S by E of Blackdown Camp and there are traces of other shafts at 600 yards W by S and 920 yards W.S.W. of the engine house. A group of silver-lead lodes are reported to have also contained white quart, silver bearing chalcocite and fluccan. The deposits were probably small. In 1847 the mine was fourteen fathoms deep (i.e. 84 feet) and raised 16 tons of lead ore (by 1850 the mine was closed).

Yellow Ochre

Yellow Ochre was used for the interior, and sometimes the exterior, decoration of cottages. It was dug up from fields in the Blackdown area and the 1839 Tithe Survey lists fields called East Ochre, West Ochre and South Ochre. There were two colours of ochre, yellow, or clay colour, and red where it had been in contact with iron deposits. It was stored and blended in part of New Barn by the Luscombes who lived in Blackdown Farmhouse near by. In the 1841 census John and Henry Luscombe of Blackdown were classified as 'Refiners of colours'. In that year John was 60 and Henry 30 years old.

John and Emma Luscombe (born between 1815 and 1818) continued as 'ochre manufacturers' during the 1850s and '60s. They had nine children and lived in the farmhouse, just 100 yards from the barn. William Elliott recalled that as a youth in the early 1870s after cutting furze on Blackdown he often came back that way to buy some delicious boiled sweets which Emma made.

Another near relative of the family, George Roger King Luscombe (born 30 December 1818), was a tailor in Loddiswell and he married Susannah Steer. They had six children and the family moved to Mill Street, Kingsbridge, soon after 1900, where Herbert, one of the sons, had a paint shop. He later moved to 19 Fore Street where he continued the business with his son under the name of H. Luscombe and Son. At the end of the 20th century the business still trades under that name and is in the capable hands of Keith Roper, his great-grandson.

John and Emma Luscombe's Farmhouse where they began their yellow ochre business.

Chapter 10: Stanton, A Deserted Village

Stanton (formerly Staunton), lies about two miles north-west of the village of Loddiswell. The early topographers spoke of the parish as being composed of two villages, Staunton and Loddiswell. In 1413 the Parsonage and Glebe lands were situated mid way between the two villages, and remained so until a new rectory was built at Loddiswell in the 1950s. Today, the only visual remains of the old Staunton village are broken pieces of cottage walling (*below*) and occasional garden plants. The surrounding land is now farmed by the Sampsons of Lilwell and Woolston Farm.

King Edgar's Sorley Charter of 992 shows that the parish boundary line 'skirted Staunton, and ran along Blackwell, or Black Pool, which is a boggy land' (now Stanton Moor and Andrew's Wood). Documentary evidence supports the statement that there was a medieval settlement at Stanton, and that it remained inhabited until the end of the 19th century.

In 1262 the Lordship of Loddiswell was in the hands of Eva de Cantilupe who, in her widowhood, gave 100 acres of land in her manor of 'Lodeswell' to the church of St Mary, Studley and the canons there, for the soul of her husband William. Over 20 names appear in the Charter Rolls, some at Stanton – 'Martin de Staunton held a ferlong of land, Edith held a ferlong.' Sampson of that time appears to have paid 15d. in rent and Studley received the rents until the Dissolution.

In 1557 'Katherine Champernown, widow, late wife of Philip Champernown, knight, and Arthur Champernown, knight, together received a grant of lands in Webberton in Loddiswell'. They were named as 'late of Studley Priory, Co. Warwick'.

A survey of Loddiswell in 1602/3 was made by Richard Tremayne and Edward Furlong for John Arundell of Lanherne. Arundell was Lord of the Manor of 'Lodswell' which included parts of Stanton. Among the freeholders was 'Hellen Carswell, wydowe who holdeth certain lands in free socage and payeth to the Lord 1s.0d. and two suites of courte'. The customary tenants included John Cawker (55) who farmed 32 acres and 'held a tenement in Staunton and one furlonge of land there by the rent of 18s.6d.' Symon Dery, also 55, had 32 acres and had 'A tenement in Staunton containing one farlinge, by the rent of 26s.11d., and hath pasture for one beast in stonland. Walter Wyett hath pasture for one beast'.

Most of these people had lived through the traumatic experiences of 1590 described in the Parish Register as 'Ye plague tyme'. The Wyetts had lost several family members to this terrible disease which seemed to spread during the warmer summer weather. The poorer cottages were small and overcrowded with often only one downstairs room about 10 feet square. Upstairs the chamber of the same size was low under a thatched roof and the earth or water closet (toilet) was at the end of the garden near the pigsty. Inside the kitchen door would be a wad of straw to clean their boots. Drinking water was fetched by all cottagers from the open well near the steam. Such were the conditions in which cottagers and their three or four children lived and normally survived.

Eight people are named as paying rent for 'Staunton moores' in the Carew rental for the Manor of Webberton dated 1676 and in the replies to Dean Milles' queries about 1750, Loddiswell is recorded as having 50 houses and Stanton 26. The overseers' accounts for Loddiswell show that money was constantly being paid out for the repair of roads at and to Stanton village:

> 1801   Paid Mr Friend bill for stones and work done in Staunton village 11s.6d.
> 1803   Pd. Mr Denbow for making 64 yards of road in Staunton Hill at 7s.6d. per yard £24.
>   Pd. Mr Hewett for 20 yards of roade in Staunton at 2s.6d. per yard £2.10s.
> 1806-7 Pd Mr Bond bill for making a road at Staunton village £2.2s.3d.

A document gives the measurements of all the parish roads and states 'Staunton Lane from Fernhill Cross to Staunton Brook 1 mile – 28 poles. Staunton Village 2 furlongs.'

From 1750 to 1841 the number of houses dropped from 26 to 12 but it would appear that the village was thriving by 1846, for in that year the Peek family were instrumental in building Stanton Bible Christian Chapel which enjoyed good attendance until the agricultural population declined and moved away in the late 1800s.

The cottage hearth.

The clapper bridge and well, Stanton village (photographed 1995).

The Plague

The plague first started in the late summer of 1348 at Weymouth, brought in from abroad by rats that escaped from the cargo ships. Epidemics surged and declined through the 15th and 16th centuries and were often traced to the local south-west ports of Teignmouth, Dartmouth and Plymouth. It was a form of typhus carried by fleas on the rats, who injected their poison into the human bloodstream. Black swellings and boils appeared with death occurring within one or two days.

The Parish Register in 1590 records the deaths in the villages of Stanton and Loddiswell, and the parish generally:

ANO 1590 Ye Plague Tyme

The 16 day of March was buried John Coombe.
The 2 day of Aprill was buried Thomas Ryder.
The- day of Aprill was buried Anthony Blake.
The same day was buried Margaret ye daughter of Robert Pytt.
The 11 of Aprill was buried Joane ye daughter of Anthony Blake.
The 18 Aprill was buried Elizabeth ye daughter of Christine Ryder.
The 20 Aprill was buried Thomazin Flashman.
The same day was buried Joan ye daughter of Thomas Woolson.
The same day was buried Ursula Browen.
The 3 of Maye was buried Christian ye daughter of Richard Chiswill.
The 8 of Maye was buried Christian Wyett.
The 20 of Maye was buried John Pytt the elder.
The same day was buried Sybil ye wyfe of James Coome.
The 21 of Maye was buried Robert ye sonne of Robert Wyett.
The 26 of Maye was buried Brydye ye wyfe of ye sonne of Robert Wyett.
The 27 of Maye was buried Agnise ye wyfe of Robert Cooke.
The 28 of Maye was buried Thomas Cooke ye elder.
The 28 of Maye was buried Simon ye sonne of Christian.
The 29 of Maye was buried Margaret Millerd.
The 30 of Maye was buried Walter Lucraft.
The same day was buried Mary ye daughter of Robert Wyett.
The 31 of Maye was buried Richard ye sonne of Thomas Averye.
The 5 of June was buried Jane ye wyfe of the same Thomas.

The 6 of June was buried John ye sonne of John Lucraft.
The 7 of June was buried Elizabeth widdo.
The 8 of June was buried Joane Coyett.
The 10 of June was buried Christine Week.
The 18 of June was buried Henrye ye sonne of the aforesaid Christian Week
The same day was buried Robert Wyett the elder
The same day was buried John Pytt the younger.
The 15 of June was buried Edmund Prydywe.
The 16 of June was buried Margaret Pytt.
The 19 of June was buried Thomas ye sonne of Anthony Downe.
The 21 of June was buried Thomas ye sonne of William Middleton.
The same day was buried Michael ye sonne of Anthony Downe.
The 22 of June was buried Henry the sonne of the same Anthony.
The 24 of June was buried Joane Dering.
The 25 of June was buried Arthure ye sonne of Milly Middleton.
The 26 of June was buried Henry Elliott
The 27 of June was buried James Middleton.
The 28 of June was buried Robert Stabb the elder.
The 1 of July was buried James ye sonne of Jeffery Langmead.
The 20 of July was buried Joane ye wyff of Christopher Wyett.
The 22 of July was buried Seth Myll.
The 29 of July was buried Michele ye daughter of Hugh Harrye.
The 15 of August was buried ? Wyett.
The 17 of August was buried Joane Wyett the younger.
The 29 of August was buried Thomasine Wyett.
The 12 of September was buried Elizabeth the last daughter of Thomas Yeoman. Finis.
The 27 of September was buried Susan Kennes.
The 22 of November was buried John the son of John Phillipp.
The 2 of February was buried Baldon Gardener.

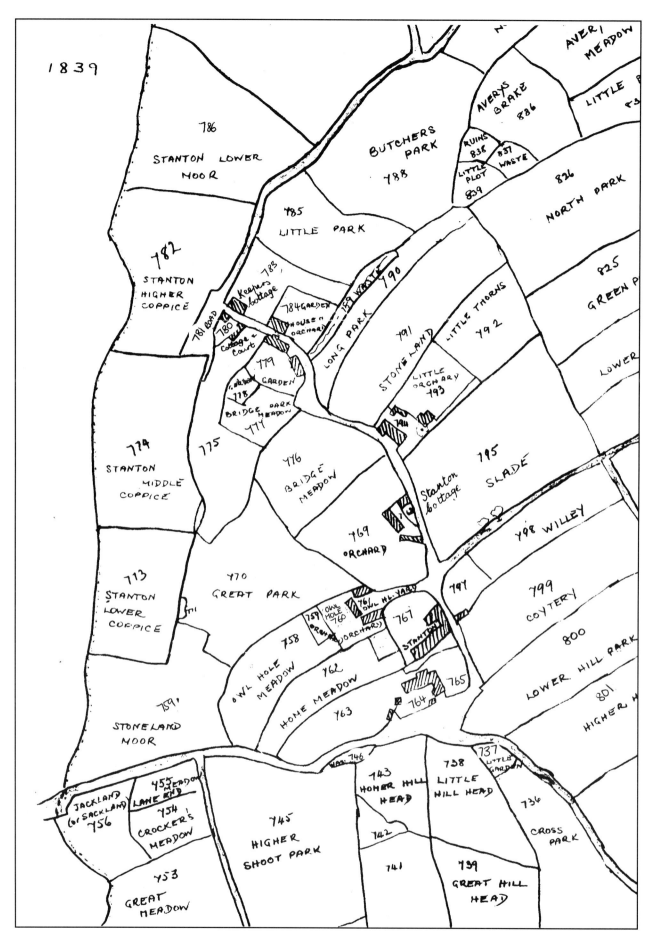

Map of Andrew's Wood area from the Tithe map of 1839

Chapter 11: Education

Sites of several early schools have been established and include Corner House in the Courtledge (*bottom right*) where the schoolroom was in an upstairs room approached by outside steps. Another early site was adjoining the Church House Inn (no longer in existence) near the site of Storridge Farm. Both were within a few yards of the Church. The Independents (later the Congregational Church) appear to have attended school in a house in Fore Sweet on the corner of Chapel Lane.

After endowing Loddiswell with a new chapel (now the Congregational Church) in Fore Sweet in 1864, Richard Peek (1782-1867) looked to education. He had already established a reading room in 1839 and his provision of a school, coming a dozen years before the 1870 Education Act, has been oft commented upon for revealing his great foresight. A British School (*below*) was built in 1853 for the sum of £1500 and endowed for £30 per year by Richard Peek (who also made some payments for the poorer children). Early admissions date from 1855 and not only was a school provided but also a house for a schoolmaster with a cottage next to it (*see page 75*).

Until 1870 the Church had its school in part of the Church House Inn property of the Arundell feoffees. However, this room was above a pigsty and clearly not suitable at all. Richard Peek was building the British School at the other end of the village and people were beginning to expect better accommodation. In the spring of 1870, following the passing of the Education Act, it was resolved by six of the feoffees that:

A portion not exceeding a quarter of an acre of Feoffee orchard be granted in trust for Schools for the education of the poor and for no other purpose whatever.

The way was clear for the building of a new National

Above right: Loddiswell British School, built in 1853 (now the primary school).

Right: One of the first schools in 1850 on the left of Corner House (photographed c.1910).

School. The task was paid for by public subscription and farmers carried stone from the Loddiswell quarry free of charge.

There was bickering between the two schools and the parish enjoyed the privilege of an open market in education. Children would move between schools for the slightest of reasons and this invariably infuriated the headmasters for salaries depended on 'payment by results' and maintaining a good attendance average. Various reasons have been documented as to why there was such movement between the two establishments. One family, for example, did not receive a Sunday School prize and others moved on just before a Sunday School tea. Rebellious children moved when punished.

It was not until 1916 that an opportunity came to unite the two schools. Although an HMI Report of 1874 had pointed out the unnecessary expense of maintaining the two schools, nothing was acted upon. Each school felt itself to be a

Headmaster John Tapp and Alice Yalland with class at the Church School, 1900.

Loddiswell British School pupils, 1875. Headmaster, Mr John Angel Attwooll (1874-83) and Assistant, Miss Mary Jane Weeks (1875-82, later Mrs Richard West).

spiritual necessity to the parish and it is to this end that they both flourished. It has also been said that the two masters, John Tapp (National) and Frederick Parker (British), by serving simultaneously and faithfully for so many years, kept the two schools separate. The County acted in the summer of 1916 to amalgamate the schools and the British School was chosen to house them.

The National School building continued to be used for social purposes, and today's villagers know it as the Village Hall. In 1937 it was used again as a classroom for Loddiswell Primary School Infants and this continued for 19 years except for a short period during the Second World War. An extra classroom was added to the present building in 1956, thus ending the daily trek for the infants to the other end of the village. A year later saw the addition of a canteen but sadly meals are no longer cooked on the premises. In 1991 a fine extension to our Primary School was officially opened.

A swimming pool was built with the help of the Parents, Teachers and Friends Association (PTFA) in 1976 with the village children enjoying many happy years swimming both in term time and in the long summer holidays. This has not been possible in the last few years so the pool was dismantled and the site cleared during the winter of 1997/8. The site is being re-developed as a play area and was the focus for much of the PTFA fund-raising for 1998-99.

The secret to any school's success lies in its staff and Loddiswell has been blessed over the years with many dedicated professionals, some staying only briefly, others devoting their whole professional life to serving our community. Mention has already been given to John Tapp and Frederick Parker. Two very important stalwarts were the Misses Common and Michell, who together oversaw the primary education of many of today's villagers. Their mantle has been passed on to today's caring staff.

Below: British School's headmaster's house, c.1927.

Logbooks survive to re-count the days of school and education in Loddiswell. Christian Michell notes in her booklet, *Schools and Education in Loddiswell* (1970), that such logbooks are a great source of social history. We can learn of wages, for example, that in 1909 Mr and Mrs John Tapp rec-

Schoolchildren in New Road, 1907.

eived the sum of £6.14s.7d. per month and this was increased to £90 a year in 1910. Alongside accounts of physical difficulties (smoking chimneys, broken doors repaired by pupils!), we read of teaching methods and subjects, examinations and visits by inspectors and local dignitaries as well as parish affairs:

1881 Smallpox in neighbourhood
1893 Typhoid fever made its appearance in Well Street.
1926 List of cases of mumps sent to Medical Officer
1927 Measles outbreak – 34 cases reported. Attendance down to 41%.

As in many country areas the work in the fields took precedence over everything else:

1873 Elder children away 'picking ears'.
1880 Sophia and Jane Hine left to go to the mill.
1887 Many children employed in fields at this season of sowing barley and planting potatoes.

The weather (typically) features prominently in logbook accounts:

Blizzard of 1891. The storm which came on last evening proved to be the most terrible known for many years. The roads are all blocked with immense drifts of snow so that no children came to school. It is in consequence closed for the remainder of the week.
1923. Torrential rain this morning only 59 present out of 90. These wet mornings spoil my percentage which otherwise is relatively high (98%).

Items about the wars also appear:

1900 Half holiday in honour of General Buller's relief of Ladysmith
1938 Gas masks fitted

Serving Education in the Parish

Above: Charles A. Bryant, headmaster 1926-31.

Top right: Concert given by pupils at Geoff Loader's retirement as headteacher (1970-92).

Above: Paul Wright's retirement from the post of headteacher (1992-97).

Above right: Presentation by Captain W. Peek to Margaret Common on her retirement as headteacher (1936-70).

Right: Christian Michell, teacher at Loddiswell School (1935-72), sitting on her presentation seat on the occasion of her retirement.

The Church School, later the Village Hall and School House, built in 1872.

September 4 1939 Staff reported for duty. School closed until further notice owing to declaration of war.

As times have changed so have the subjects taught in our school. Logbooks for the National School chronicle boys taking up wood carving and girls knitting woollens for the soldiers in the First World War. We noted earlier that the focus for PTFA fundraising in 1998-99 was a small garden area. Back in 1926 a special subject of gardening was introduced to the curriculum – the boys were to grow vegetables in an allotment and the girls were to cultivate flowers in the school garden. Inspections for gardening and rural science took place in 1929. Sport was a feature back in October 1925 when the head noted in the logbook of the day, 'Assembled school at 1pm today to enable a football team to journey to Aveton Gifford to play a football match after the afternoon session'. Sport continues to flourish. We still play against Aveton Gifford as well as other local schools, and cricket is also enjoyed. A dance club meets on Tuesdays after school, has represented the school at area and county level and put on a performance at the Devon County Show in May 1998. Music is and always has been an important subject and is enjoyed by all pupils. Adhering to the demands of the National Curriculum means that some subjects disappear or reappear with a new name.

In an age when we regularly read in the daily press of threatened school closures, Loddiswell Primary School continues to flourish. It has a high reputation amongst its peers and is looking forward to providing a good education for the new millennium. Long may it continue!

The school has a clear sense of purpose and direction and is focusing on raising attainment and standards and providing an effective learning environment... The ethos of the school reflects the school's commitment to high achievement, a good learning environment, equality of opportunity and good relationships.

HMI OFSTED Report, May 1998

LODDISWELL PRE-SCHOOL

Loddiswell Pre-School was formed in May 1977 to meet the needs of the growing community in Loddiswell. It is run voluntarily by a Management Committee of parents whose children attend the Pre-School. Over the years it has had several supervisors, including Sue Gallagher, Frank Prowse, Denise Lethbridge and Lisa Farleigh.

When the Pre-School first began it held one or two sessions a week but now opens four times a week. Three sessions are held on Monday, Wednesday and Friday mornings in the Village Hall for children aged three to five and one session is held at Loddiswell Primary School for those aged four to five, the Early Years' Group. This gives the children a good opportunity to familiarise themselves with the school before they begin full time.

Loddiswell Pre-School also runs a Parent and Toddler Group on Wednesday mornings in the Congregational Church Hall. This caters for parents with children of a younger age before they begin the Pre-School sessions.

Teacher Bessie Lakeman and class, 1908.
(Left to right) back: R. Stone, F. Hine, N. Rogers, D. Hine, ?, S. Guest;
centre: A. Hine, J. Guest, R. Watts, S. Newman, A. Rundle, M. Baker, B. Hine;
front: S. Guest, G. Brooking, C. Hingston, M. Tolchard, A. West, F. Watts, I. Guest (in front).

Loddiswell School, 1920.
(Left to right) back: Albert Kendall, Bill Brooking, Bert Watts, ?, Tom Hendin, ?,
?, Bert Brown;
centre: Bill Stone, Eveline Hine, Dulcie Farmer, Arthur Hingston, Dorothy Sherrell, Gladys Sherrell,
Bill Luscombe, Jim Hine, Ted Guest;
front: Bert Watts, Arthur Hine, Kathleen Freeman, Tom Brooking.

Miss Evans and class, 1924/5.
(Left to right) back: Walter Kernick, Horace Martin, Jack Freeman, Fred Edgecombe, Stanley Hine, ?, ?,
John (Bill) Horton;
centre: Miss Evans, George Skinner, Bill Stone, Bill Reeves (Churchstow), Herbert Yeoman, Sydney Jeffery;
front: Queenie Hine, Kathleen Freeman, Helen Freeman, Marion Ryder, Dorothy Luscombe, ? Newman,
Daphne Hingston, Ivy Hosking, ?, Georgette Brooking, Hazel Hingston, ? Reeves, Flora Horton.

Henry Clement Sargent and pupils, 1924/5.
(Left to right) back: Tom Brooking, Jim Hine, Bill Brooking, Bill Luscombe, Alphonso Hine, Ben Freeman,
Harold Joint, Bert Watts, Ted Guest, Horace Rudell;
centre: Henry Clement Sargent, Harold Webber, Alfred Goss, Alan Baker, Francis Kendall, Walter Hine,
Horace Maynard, ?, Arthur Hine, Albert Kendall, Bert Brown;
front: Harold Skinner, George Skinner, Doris Joint, Margary Sandover, Beatrice Goss, Nelly Sandover,
Dulcie Farmer, Emily Hine, Eveline Harding, ?, Tom Hendin.

Thomas Higman, headmaster (1931-33), with his class in 1932.
(Left to right) back: Alan Roberts, Evelyn Pile, Alice Yalland, Joan Brooking, Doll Ryder, Nellie Horton,
Gladys Fishburn, Leslie Sampson, Mr Higman;
centre: Muriel Stoyle, Jack Hine, Ronald Stone, Marjorie Brooking, Evelyn Brooking, Chris Ryder,
Fred Widger, Dolly Yabsley;
front: Glyn Brooking, Roy Brooking, Gordon Taylor, Georgie Roberts, Stanley Goss.

Miss Ethel Whitell and her class, 1933.
(Left to right) back: Miss Whittell, Howard Harris, Chloe Shephard, Alice Taylor, Irene Preston, Ivan Pope,
Sandford Jeffery;
3rd row: Reg Sampson, Doris Pile, Pearl Brooking, Mary Bennett, Rosie Hine, Margaret Soper, Sheila Taylor,
Phyllis Elliott, Cora Ryder;
2nd row: Cyril Fred Brooking, Horace Camp, Cyril Brooking, Herbert Harvey, Bill Creber, Harold Pope,
Arthur Brooking;
front: Ted Quick, Brian Duffty, Alfred Rowe, Bill Seldon, Philip Hine.

Ann Willis and class, 1978.
(Left to right) back: Simon Carter, Martin Jeffery, Martyn Wills, Paul Janes, Neil Hockin, Justin James,
Phillip Ward, Simon Kemsley;
centre: Claire Waterhouse, Ann Carpenter, Rebecca Cater, Alison Ibbetson, Rachel Wilson, Natalie Johns,
Rebecca Hart, Wendy Parkes, Sarah Rogers, Tanya Ryder;
front: Simon Sweet, Emma Lewis, Paulette Thomas, Stephanie Collins, Steven Welham.

Miss Steele's Class 1, 1984.
(Left to right) back: Jenny Cater, Kate Murphy, Tricia Hilton, Jesse Burrows, Michelle Bortoszyn, Adrian Hall,
Lucy Slaughter;
centre: Kelly Lethbridge, Emma Oliphant, Jacqueline Hallam, Catherine Herring, Charlotte Bowen,
William Davies, Christopher Hall, Sarah Lethbridge;
front: Lewis Winzer, Jennifer Sercombe, Julia Sweeney, Daniel Stathers, Richard Schaefer, Jane Broda,
Tom Cook, Mark Sampson, Francesca Bortoszyn, Katie Beer.

Teachers and pupils of Loddiswell School, 1981.

(Left to right) back: Alison Ibbetson, Simon Carter, Martyn Wills, Wendy Parkes, Neil Hockin, Rebecca Cater, Natalie Johns, Rachael Wilson, Paul Janes, Phillip Ward, Jason Perring, Rebecca Hart, Simon Kemsley, Martin Jeffery, Kirsty Broda;

4th row: Stephanie Collins, Kirsten Holt, Kevin Brooking, Helen Rockey, Bernice Hine, Paulette Thomas, Emma Lewis, Jonathan Hinton, Peter Hosking, Catherine Ward, Steven Welham, Tanya Ryder, Clare Waterhouse, Diane Jeffery, Ann Carpenter, Stephen Harvey, Julie Hinder, Simon Sweet;

3rd row: Catherine Penwill, Jamie Carter, Clive Parkes, Robert Wills, Helen Ibbetson, Nicholas Rockey, Mark Eastley, Andrew Hosking, Karen White, Simon Wilson, Sally Wigg, Elsa Kelly, Mark Yeoman, Catherine Cater, Shaun Hart, Clare Jeffery, Benjamin Kemsley, Gemma Hallam, Douglas Harvey;

2nd row: Benjamin Slaughter, Kate Stathers, Donna Pethybridge, Natalie Collins, Suzanne Hine, Mrs Garland, Mrs Hart, Mr Loader, Mrs Tolchard, Mrs Willis, Mrs Harvey, Sarah Holt, James Hurst, Celeste Mutton, Richard White, Lynne Yeoman, Clare Ward;

front: Beverley Eastley, Neil Hart, Ben Cook, Ian Ibbetson, Glyn Hine, Robin Sadler, Susan Hinder, Melanie Lucket, Paul Bowen, Richard Knight, Nigel Edgcombe, Jonathan Cater.

Mrs Kath Tolchard's Class 2, 1984.
(Left to right) back: Andrew Rose, Hannah Slaughter, Neil Hart, Ben Cook, Gareth Janes, Glyn Hine,
Ian Ibbetson, Beverley Eastley, Andrew Beer;
centre: Richard Knight, Paul Bowen, Melanie Luckett, Jonathan Wigg, Ben Slaughter, Katie Allen,
Lynne Yeoman, Clare Herring;
front: Christopher Sweeney, Nicola Hallam, Jonathan Cater, Nigel Edgcombe, Tim Davies, Susan Hinder,
Claire Eastley, Clare Sampson, Carolyn Hine, Amy Holt, Kirsty Luckett.

Miss Jill Hart's Class 3, 1984.
(Left to right) back: Suzanne Hine, Ben Kemsley, Gemma Hallam, Nicholas Rockey, Claire Jeffery,
Catherine Cater, Shaun Hart, Helen Ibbetson, Catherine Penwill;
centre: Elsa Kelly, Mark Eastley, Sally Wigg, Kirsten Allen, Neil Hocking, Andrew Hosking, Jane Sercombe,
Mark Yeoman, Robert Beer;
front: Kate Stathers, Justin Weeks, Jamie Carter, Sarah Wootton, Natalie Collins, Douglas Harvey,
James Hurst, Sarah Holt.

Mrs Linda Fairfax's Class 1, 1990.
(Left to right) back: Mark Blight, Peter Ellis, Mark Pope, Anna Prowse, Vicky Heath, Zoe Brooking,
Robert Weeks, Katie Rose, Tim Lethbridge, Robert Woollam;
centre: Amy Widger, Katie Yellin, Annabel Lethbridge, Jessica Brown, Hannah Punchard, Holly Marshall,
Michael Dusting;
front: Tanya Reeve, Anne-Marie Hainsworth.

Mrs Gill Hart's Class 2, 1990.
(Left to right) Andrew Burner, Angela Jones, Jenny Yellin, Robert Lethbridge, Daniel Fisher, Simon Pope,
Ben Hudson, Hannah Marshall, Annette Sercombe, Rebecca Wootton;
centre: Claire Dusting, Emma Lethbridge, Carla Murphy, Amy Hart, Andrew Reeve, Clare Fairfax,
Sarah Sweet, Caroline Schaefer;
front: Anna-Marie Blight, Peter Hinton, Tim Stathers, Sam and Jack Luttman, Zoe Cater, Danielle Bradley.

Mr Geoff Loader's Class 3, 1990.
(Left to right) back: Craig Wallis, Victoria Punchard, Poppy Wallis, Julia Sweeney, Mark Sampson;
centre: Cheryl Jones, Katie Beer, Daniel Pettitt, Helen Fairfax, Jenny Sercombe, Richard Schaefer,
Lucy Slaughter, Emma Brooking, James Fisher;
front: Verity Moffat, Vicky Heath, Katie Hine, Stephen Whitfield, Martin Dusting, Jenny Lethbridge, Sarah
Smith, Lewis Winzer (front left), Ashley Winzer (front right).

Mrs Lin Fairfax's Class 1, 1998.
(Left to right) back: Michael Fischer, Jonathan Coyte, Jessica Martin, Phillipa Hyne, Chloe Harvey,
Amy Elliott, Laura Taylor, Edmund Withnell, Troy Prout;
3rd row: Ella Yabsley, Mrs Margaret Hole, Karl Hollingsworth, Hayley Monk, Kate Harvey, Thomas Ashby,
Helen Dyke, Craig Cheney, Thomas Bennett, Rhys Widger;
2nd row: Louise George, Laura Purcell, Jessica Edgcombe, Lucy Widger, Natasha Hyne,
Daniel Murry, Mrs Sue Slaughter;
front: Alex Slade, Charlie Gocher, Freddie Wiggett, Toby Oldrieve, James Montague, Edward Danby, James Taylor.

Mrs Judith Holden's Class 2, 1998.
(Left to right) back: Rachel Treeby, Jasmine Bradley, Sarah Montague, Louise Clarke, Anya Trounce,
Daniel Taylor, Thomas Hoey, Thomas Martin;
3rd row: Marc Townsend, Sophie Elliott, Rosie Woodham, James Hyne, Nicola Widger, Christopher King,
Sarah Coyte, Craig McCormick;
2nd row: Mrs Judith Holden, Gregory Down, Phoebe Bocchinelli, Lauren Slade, Rachel George, Katie Hodge,
Georgia Johnson, Miss Katie Hine;
front: Ben Hunt, Timothy Little, Edward Ashby, Robert Dyke, Luke Oldrieve.

Mrs Viv Clare's Class 3, 1998
back: Hayley McCormick, Ashley Treeby, Jack Elliott, Lana Widger, Gemma Matthews, Toby Jones,
Molly Ashby;
3rd row: Rachael Woollam, Rebecca Little, Ashley Commons, Marcus Rossi, Julian Hainsworth,
Jack Ballinger, Charlotte Hyne, Abigail Heath;
2nd row: Mrs Viv Clare, Jack Howden, Fiona Gallagher, Daisy Ballinger, Rachel Harvey, Sarah Hudson, Dawn
Pettitt, Mrs Cath Littlejohn;
front: Alex Hollingsworth, Jack Bennett, Charlie Yabsley, Louis Johnson, Andrew Herbert-Read, Peter Wood.

Chapter 11: Transport and Communications

Until the end of the 18th century South Devon was a mainly rural area with small villages and isolated houses. Fields were on average two to five acres divided by earth banks. Cottages had large vegetable gardens or allotments and the communities were largely self sufficient. Produce for sale or barter was carried by pack-horse teams between the towns and villages along tracks which kept, where possible, to the higher ground to avoid the soft, boggy areas. The nearest town to Loddiswell, however, was Kingsbridge, lying three miles away over the River Avon which had to be crossed.

James Green gave the width of the pack-horse bridge at Hatch in 1665 as six-and-a-half feet and remarked that the 'Bridge is very old and out of repair'.

The other bridge over the Avon recorded by Benjamin Donn in his survey in 1765 was the Avon Mill Bridge, then 6 feet wide, providing an alternative way to Kingsbridge past Wrinkley, Slade and Belle Hill. Fruit from the Canary Islands brought into the Kingsbridge Estuary by ocean-going schooners and fertiliser from South America were pack-horsed along this route with wool and barley being returned to port

Both these bridges were widened when wheeled transport became common; Avon Mill Bridge being widened by 2 feet upstream in 1809 and Hatch Bridge in 1827 by 2 feet on each side for the improved road from Aveton Gifford to the new Turnpike Road near Rake Farm.

The Turnpike Trust set up in 1823, had worked on the road from Sorley to Rake and in 1827 undertook the cutting of a new road through Fosse's Copse to Loddiswell. A new bridge was built over the Avon but without, apparently, much thought paid to its design – it collapsed almost immediately! A Kingsbridge lecturer in 1879 commented: 'I recollect the falling of the bridge that crosses the Avon at Loddiswell. It had just been finished and very few people had crossed it before it fell.' Perhaps it was a little ambitious at that time to construct a single elliptical arch with a span of 51 feet but it did not take long for the bridge to be rebuilt.

Before the Turnpike was cut up through the hillside from Loddiswell Bridge to the village, the

Road to Yanston Bridge

pedestrian and pack-horse track was a little further upstream and crossed the Avon at New Mill (formerly Hambley's or Willing's Mill). A survey in 1665 reported 'Bridge in decay' and many years later Mr Arthur Hingston recalled from his childhood that one of the routes from Kingsbridge was 'up Darky Lane, by Easter Field Barn, on to Leigh, then to Miller's Path, around by Rake's Farm House, over the ford at Willing's Mill and up the steep hill to Loddiswell'. The present bridge of three segmental arches is much newer than Avon Mill Bridge and Hatch Bridge and did not need to be widened. It was built in 1893 and in order to avoid confusion with the Turnpike 'New Bridge' it acquired the name of 'New Mill Bridge'.

When the Kingsbridge Road Station was opened on the South Devon Railway at Wrangaton in 1848, Robert Foale established a coach service from the Kings Arms, Kingsbridge, through Loddiswell to Wrangaton. By 1880 there were 36 coaches a week on the route with a change of horses available at Stile Cottage. Although the road had been improved there were steep hills to be negotiated and it put a great strain on the horses. Their average working life was not more than seven years and in 1893 six horses died in as many weeks on this route.

Most rural roads, except for the turnpikes, were still very rough and stones for their repair were quarried locally and hauled by horse and cart to various sites to be broken by hand. Ken Hyne remembers as a very young boy, riding with his father J.W. Hyne who would tender to the Parish Council for fetching the stone from the quarries with his horse and cart. The stone came from quarries at Idestone and Blackdown and, as there was no way of weighing it, a member of the Council would fill wooden boxes each holding a cubic yard of stone. A tally was kept by the head quarryman of the number of boxes loaded into the carts and hauled to the various sites. Here they were tipped at one of the 'landings', later known as 'chipping dumps'. Landings in Loddiswell Parish were at Ham and Loddiswell Butts, at the top of Town's Lane, at Muckwell Hill and at Churchland Green. Tom Luscombe and his son Earnest sat crossed legged on a sack of straw using hammers to break the stone into

Above: Topsham Bridge, originally a pack-horse bridge, was widened on both sides in 1820 to 15 feet.

Above left: Richard West, carrier between Loddiswell and Kingsbridge, and his wife Mary Jane West (née Weeks) who taught at Loddiswell School (1875-82).

Above: The Turnpike Toll House at Sorley.

Left: 'Crossing Hatch Bridge on the improved road from Aveton Gifford to Rake which was widened in 1827.

Above: New Mill Bridge built in 1893.

approximately 2 inch pieces, known as quartering, ready for the steam roller gangs to repair the roads.

THE STONEBREAKERS' SONG

In the year 1800, I think in sixteen
In the month of December with frost sharp and clean
When trade it was poor and the prices were low
In search of farm labour away I did go.
For want of sustenance my mind did compel
To join a stone quarry near to Loddiswell
For to break, wheel and carry as I understood
The wages were poor but the money was good.

We entered our name then to work did repair
Each man got a shilling a day for his share.
Some breaking, some wheeling, some carrying stones,
Allowing that small fish is better than none.
With a set of brave fellows right true in real life
We wrought in this quarry from morning to night.
Then answered our names as they came in the list
Each man got his wages paid down in his fist.

On the third day we wrought it began a New Year
Which made 1817 to appear.
Each man took his station and answered his name,
But a great alteration were wrought by the rain.
We were all dismissed next day to appear,
For which our brave master deserves a loud cheer.
That paid down our wages and let us go home
In bright shining pages his praise I'll make known.

The Brent to Kingsbridge Railway was opened in 1893 reducing the road traffic at that time. Rail freight reached its peak in the war years 1939-45 and then gradually declined until the line was closed in 1963. National Motorways, begun in the late 1950s and early '60s by Ernest Marples, Minister of Transport, encouraged the use of larger and faster articulated lorries, and by 1995 these were allowed to carry up to 44 tons.

Cars have become a necessity in a rural community where the public transport services have declined, and with many parishioners now commuting to work. The one or two cars in the parish in the early 1930s multiplied to one, and often two per household by the late '90s.

Devon County Council's Highways statistics collated in 1996 show that in Loddiswell Parish there were: 54 households with no car, 194 with one car, 88 households with two, 23 households with three or more. There was a total of 443 cars for 853 persons living in 359 households. On average there were 2.4 persons and 1.2 cars per household.

Much of the weekly shopping can be done at the supermarkets of Tesco, Somerfield, Sainsbury's, Safeway and Asda, where car parking is free and convenient but this has reduced the viability of the High Street shops which are now often occupied by estate agents and charities.

Right: Loddiswell Bridge well buttressed.

Workmen and steamroller by New Mill Bridge, c.1920.

Yanston Bridge built by George Steer in 1815 for £15.10s.

POST OFFICE

After 55 years the Post Office at Loddiswell moved from James Harvey's house at Mount Pleasant (Prospect Cottage) to the Fore Street office (part of Elliotts). George Yalland, a shoemaker there in 1893, became the Postmaster and Loddiswell continued to receive its mail from Totnes until 1896. The village then became a 'Railway Sub-office' (RSO) and was serviced by a horse and cart travelling between South Brent and Kingsbridge. Later, mail came direct to Loddiswell Station.

Telephonic communications from the village to Kingsbridge began in 1897, in the form of telegrams or 'wires'. Susie Kennard became Postmistress and, on retirement, lived with her brother Jim at Quarry Park. In 1915 William Bush married Dorothy Clayton, the Postmistress, and later Molly Bush helped in the Post Office. This had become a time-consuming job as all the

Right: W.J. Guest's van c.1920 with passenger Wilfred Taylor.

Below: Telegraph and money order Post Office Staff, c.1915. Left to right: William Preston (Bill), John Hendy, Bob Skinner, Postmaster George Yalland (behind), Joe Chamberlain.

incoming calls had to be connected to the appropriate subscribers with a plug on the switch-board. Automatic connections superseded this system and in the 1980s fibre-optic cables were laid throughout the UK. These allowed a large number of messages to be relayed simultaneously.

The advances in technology since the mid-20th century have been phenomenal. Mobile phones provide instant contact at work or leisure whenever the need arises. Developments in computers have also been rapid – through the miniaturisation of the components and the linking of the systems throughout the world on the internet.

Timber frame for the Silveridge Rail Bridge, 1892.

Loddiswell Station.

Brent To Kingsbridge Railway

When the Bristol and Exeter Railway had been extended to Wrangaton in 1848 and to Plymouth in 1849, Robert Foale decided to change his stage-coach route. Instead of competing on the Kingsbridge to Plymouth journey he would open up a route from Kingsbridge, through Loddiswell along the Turnpike road to the new Kingsbridge Road Station at Wrangaton, where his brother-in-law Charles Crispin had opened the Kingsbridge Road Hotel. Other stagecoach owners, John Tucker and Samuel Boon, soon joined or competed with him and over the years the route became very popular.

By 1880 36 coaches a week, an omnibus and a handful of delivery vans travelled along this way and it was clear that a better access to Kingsbridge was needed. This was not a new idea as plans for a rail link had been discussed on several occasions. Permission to build a branch line was passed in 1864 and in 1867 a three-mile stretch of track was laid between South Brent and Avonwick, with four further miles the following year before the company ran into debt. The scheme was renewed in 1872 but no more real progress was made until the Kingsbridge and Salcombe Company was taken over by the Great Western Railway Company 16 years later in 1888.

Top right: Steam train arrives at Loddiswell, 1921.

Right: Mark and Clare Sampson play in the snow with Bennie during the blizzard of 1986 when the main road at Muckwell Hill (north of Woolston Lodge) was completely blocked.

Below: Topsham Crossing, 1963.

Work was all set to begin in 1891 when 250 navvies were brought into the area, many from the mining towns of South Wales. One man who was living in a hut at Gara Bridge with three or four others had unfortunately brought small-pox with him. Dr Twinning found seven other cases at Modbury and promptly segregated them, sending them to an isolation ship in Plymouth Harbour.

On March 9/10 1891 a severe blizzard swept across the South West blocking roads with blinding snow in the strong easterly wind. Robert Popplestone remembered a living snowman banging on the door of his farmhouse at Blackwell

Above: Diesel car leaves Loddiswell Station, 1961.

Left: Gilbert Garland supervising the unloading of rails with Harold Reeves, Horace Fice and Fred Brooking near Sorley Tunnel.

Below: Gilbert watching Peter Carpenter straightening the track

Below left: Programme of events for the opening of the railway, 18 December 1893. Schoolchildren, the village band and inhabitants followed in procession from the school to the station. There was to be a general entertainment at the National School, followed by a free tea and fireworks.

Opening of the Railway

Programme of arrangements for Monday

1) A procession to be formed outside the British School at 11.45 am consisting of The Band – School children – Committee general inhabitants of village & locality

(N.B. The committee earnestly ask all who can to join & make the procession a success.

2) The procession will march to the Loddiswell Station and will there meet the G.W.R. Directors to whom an Address will be presented

3) A public entertainment to all school children in the National School – at 2.30 p.m.

4) A free tea to all school children in the British School at 4 p.m. to be followed by a display of fireworks. children to bring cups for tea.

N.B. All children for the procession must assemble at their respective schools at 11.30 a.m.

Parks, asking for shelter for the coach horses. The coach had left Kingsbridge at 5pm on Monday 9 March for the railway station at Wrangaton. A mile beyond Loddiswell the snow was so thick that the driver tried to persuade his passengers to allow him to turn back, but they had business appointments in Plymouth and elsewhere, and offered a bribe of 5 shillings a passenger (later increased to 10 shillings) before the driver would mount the box and drive on. One of the passengers helped him navigate but it was a hopeless task. The coach was abandoned, and the passengers struggled through the snow to the California Inn one-and-a-half miles away, where many other exhausted travellers were spending the night. Work on the railway had stopped and the navvies were glad of employment clearing the roads.

The men were familiar with harsh living conditions and their vocabulary included several crude words. The Rev. Boultbee invited the men and their Navvy Missioner to Loddiswell Church School, and addressed them at the first of many Navvy Mission Meetings. Hymns were sung to the accompaniment of the brass band under the direction of John Tapp, the headmaster.

At Court House lived Mrs Augusta Pitman, a colourful figure and a very live wire. It was she who first produced *The Mikado* in Kingsbridge and she now organised weekly concerts for all those navvies who had descended on Loddiswell and Woodleigh. She used the band and the choir, and encouraged the navvies to sing and play. On Saturday evenings a Band of Hope meeting was held. A new classroom just built in 1892 at the National School, was handed over to the navvies as a billiard and reading room.

The line was opened on 18 December 1893 amid great festivities. The *Kingsbridge Gazette* of 22 December 1893 states:

The passengers and officials met with the greatest reception at Loddiswell Station. The brass band, having marched the mile from the village, followed by the school children and general inhabitants, played lively airs as the first train ran through the station. Another loaded train started at 11.50 am and a third, carrying the Directors, General Manager, Chief Engineer and others, made a special stop at Loddiswell. After a few appropriate remarks by the Vicar and the Rector of Woodleigh the Viscount Emlyn briefly replied, expressing pleasure and surprise at the enthusiasm displayed and the reception given by the Loddiswell and Woodleigh people.

In the late 1800s and the early 1900s the railway was a key part of many local communities and train drivers had a particular standing among them. They were allowed some flexibility, so much so, that one driver kept chickens not far from the track at Loddiswell. Every day the train would be 'delayed' at Loddiswell, while he went to feed them – and time was made up with a steam regulator at full throttle on the remainder of the journey. The present owners verified this story, some years ago, when they discovered the remains of the old chicken run.

The line developed a unique 'personality' and there were many occasions when 'special arrangements' were observed. The train would sometimes make an unscheduled stop at Topsham Crossing for Martha Hine to drop off a parcel of groceries or washing for her son, Alphonso, the crossing keeper, and it was not unusual for the driver of the goods train to stop for a chat with a salmon poacher or warn him of the approaching water bailiff. One always knew when Bob Hine was driving as he would sound a 'cuckoo' on the whistle as he approached Rake cutting to let his mother in Loddiswell know he was on duty.

Many of the station masters were keen gardeners in their spare time and this was encouraged by the District Traffic Superintendent in the 1930s. The platform and surrounding flower gardens at Loddiswell were immaculately kept and won a number of competitions for the best kept station gardens. The track too was well maintained and the embankments and cuttings were also trimmed by a keen Permanent Way Gang of Loddiswell. They were proud of 'their' line and were rewarded in 1959 by winning the award for the best kept length of track in the Plymouth Division

The line was a vital link to South Devon and its greatest use was during the Second World War. In addition to the passengers, post bags, papers and milk churns being carried, the tonnage was further increased with troops and their equipment. Many extra trains were run for the troops as the invasion forces increased, and special trains were run for Generals Montgomery and Eisenhower when they came to inspect the preparations being made along the coast.

There were a few frightening experiences as well. On a dark, wet winter's evening, a German Heinkel bomber swooped low over the town of Kingsbridge and caught sight of the glowing fire box of the train travelling up towards Sorley Tunnel. Driver Dunn heard the scream of the approaching aircraft and knew they were the target. He slammed the regulator wide open and the head of steam propelled them at full speed towards the safety of the tunnel. The 500 yards seemed a long way but as they entered the tunnel an explosion was heard in the neighbouring fields.

The South Hams has a large agricultural community and had relied, to a great extent, on the railway for the haulage of produce out of, and requisites into, the area. Cattle were transported by rail in the pre-war days and during the Kingsbridge Fair Week, around 20 July, as many as 120 wagons of livestock would be loaded at the station to be hauled away by two 45xx locos.

In the autumn of 1941 sugar beet began to be loaded for shipment to the sugar factory at Kidderminster for processing. This trade built up rapidly and by the late 1950s up to 100 tons a day were being dispatched during the season.

John Westcott Ltd. of Kingsbridge, the local coal merchant, took delivery of 3000 tons of coal each year by rail until the early 1960s, and it was estimated that in 1962 the total freight on the line was in excess of 12 000 tons.

By 1963 road systems were being developed and improved for the increasing road freight vehicles and cars, and it became necessary to justify the continuing survival of a line to Dr Richard Beeching, Chairman of the British Railways Board. However, the Contracts Department at Paddington, sold the track and equipment to a firm of scrap iron merchants while negotiations were taking place to save the line. The contractor is reputed to have signed the scrap contract, allegedly for £18 000, and sold it to an Eastern European country for re-use. All hopes were dashed of preserving a line which had served the South Devon communities well for 70 years.

DARE DEVIL KIDS

In olden days boys were accustomed to creating their own amusements and Loddiswell boys were no exception. The attractive River Avon provided an excellent place for swimming at Hatch Bridge or for just stick racing down the river. Young boys were also fascinated by the train and John Marsh remembers going to Loddiswell Station with Eric Mabin, Barry Sweeney, David Quick and Gareth Haylett and hiding in the bushes opposite the station.

When the Kingsbridge to Brent train arrived they would climb aboard into an empty compartment and take a free ride to South Brent jumping off on the goods yard side as it drew into the station. After a couple of hours in South Brent they slipped back through the goods yard to take the journey home.

Did their parents know? – John Marsh says 'Gracious No! We would have been skinned alive!! because taking a FREE trip would have been dishonest.'

Navvies at Gara Bridge Station, 1893.

Chapter 12: The War Years

The 20th century has seen much suffering from the effects of war with the loss of life and material and the destruction of architectural and historic buildings. This began with with the Boer War (1899-1902). Many Loddiswell men went to South Africa during this war, including John Sparrow of Reveton Farm, who sold his farm and joined the Somerset Yeomanry.

General Sir Lewis Stratford Tollemache Halliday V.C. K.C.B. D.L. (1870-1966) came to live at The Cottage, near Loddiswell Butts, with his wife, Violet, after he retired from the Royal Marines in the 1930s. He was awarded the Victoria Cross for his leadership in defending the British Legation in Peking on 24 June 1900 against the 'Righteous Harmony Fists' (nicknamed 'The Boxers'). When Violet died in 1949 he moved away to live with his daughter Jane Sutherland.

Arthur Wellesley Wellington, the School Attendance Officer for Woodleigh and Loddiswell, came to the school in the 1950s to tell the children of his experiences during the siege of Ladysmith. His comrades called him 'The Duke' and he wrote 115 letters home giving an account of the South African campaign. On the last day of the siege he wrote, 'all the Devons volunteered for a desperate breakout, but only 100 were found to be fit enough'. He also commented 'I never regret having had these experiences, to witness the daring deeds of brave men and their self denial in trying to comfort their wounded comrades'. A school holiday was given to celebrate the Relief of Ladysmith but it is estimated that 6000 men had lost their lives in the Boer War.

When war was declared in 1914 many men volunteered, thinking the conflict would soon be over – no one was expecting, or prepared for, the enormous loss of life and suffering to come. Many soldiers fighting in the muddy trenches of the Somme in 1916 or in a sea of mud at Ypres in 1917 lost their lives. The heavy artillery guns became bogged down and their cavalry horses were killed. Of the 8.9 million men of the British Empire who were mobilised, 910 000 were wounded or killed.

James A. Michell, Christian Michell's father, wrote this letter to his brother on 2 April 1915 :

Dear Robert,

Just a line to let you know what has happened As you are aware a short while ago I got a job to go out to Northern Nigeria on an alluvial tin mine, and after a most hurried departure reached Liverpool on Friday evening last... On Saturday last the 27th ulto we were to join the ship Falaba *at the Princess Pier, Liverpool. We got aboard and the boat sailed at 6pm. On Sunday soon after 12 noon a person pointed out to me the periscope of a submarine on the water and of course excitement prevailed. Soon after this the submarine came to surface and a stern chase began in which our boat, the* Falaba, *was outdistanced. The submarine drew up parallel alongside and called upon our Commander to abandon ship, this was about 1pm. I saw the swine, five of them dressed in khaki, standing on the tower of the submarine. At this stage I went down into my cabin and after telling the other two occupants what was afoot, as they were lying down in their bunks, put on a lifebelt, went up on the top deck where the boats were slung out in readiness and jumped into a boat which was being lowered. There was no panic, at least I saw none, and our boat reached the water safely with about 35 to 40 people in it.*

The next boat however capsized owing to the block which carries the rope breaking and the occupants number perhaps 30 were precipitated into the water, a distance of say, 20 to 25 feet. I am afraid a great number of these were drowned. Another boat was smashed to matchwood against the ship and the occupants fared badly. At any rate we were lucky and got safely away and picked up some fellows who swam to us.

Just then the torpedo was fired, exactly at 1.05 pm. (as I looked at my watch) I saw the ship struck and saw human beings moving about on the decks. The Falaba *heeled over on the starboard side and in a few minutes sank stern first. The whole scene was simply fearful and hard to explain. The sea was very choppy and rough but by baling which another fellow and myself did and by the skilful efforts of an army sergeant who took charge of the boat we kept afloat. At 1.20 pm a steam drifter, the* Eileen Emma *of Lowestoft bore down upon us and we got aboard. This was a risky job as the sea was rough and we had to wait opportunity and jump and grab the handrail. A big trawler man caught me and fairly hoisted me in over with one effort and landed me on the drifter's deck face down. Then until 3pm. we cruised about picking up floats laden with people and pulling people out of the water..*

It was a horrible sight, four of the people we pulled up from the water died on our hands, one of these was the Commander of the Falaba, *we covered them over and let them lie on the deck...*

Roll of Honour
Names of the men of Loddiswell who served their King and Country during the Great War 1914-1918

Name	Rank	Unit	Front	Remarks
Allin, Harold Wyse	Lieut.	Shropshire	Palestine	Died of wounds in Palestine
Bevell, William	Corpl	RE	France	Lost leg. Awarded M.M.
Bevell, Wilfred	Private	MT	Home Service	
Brooking, Richard	Private	Devons	France	Killed in Action
Brooking, Thomas	Lieut.	Somersets	France	
Brooking, George	P.O.	Royal Navy	MS *Centurion*	
Brooking, William	Corpl	DCLI	France, Balkans & Egypt	
Brooking, Archibald	Corpl	RGA	France & Italy	
Brooking, Henry	Corpl	RGA	France	
Brooking, Arthur	Gunner	Royal Navy	MS *Achilles*	
Brown, John	Private	Glosters	France	
Brown, Philip R.	P.O.	Royal Navy	MS *Superb*	
Brown, William	P.O.	Royal Navy	HM *Moniter 32*	
Brown, Thomas	A.B.	Royal Navy	MS *Pelorom*	
Bush, William	C.P.O.	Royal Navy	MS *Tiger*	
Baker, Percy	Trooper	Surrey Yeomanry	France	
Chamberlain, John	Private	Labour Battn.	France	
Corner, Samuel	Stoker	Royal Navy	MS *New Zealand*	
Conran, W.H.B.	Captain	AS Corps	France	
Davis, JoIm	Corpl.	AS Corps	France	
Eastley, William	Stoker	Royal Navy	MS *Indefatigable*	Killed Jutland Battle
Eastley, John	Corpl.	Devons	France & Mesopotamia	Wounded twice
Eastley, Norman	Private	Devons	France	Wounded
Eastley, Herbert	Stoker	Royal Navy	MS *Aurora*	
Elliott, William	Gunner	RGA	Palestine	
Edgcumbe, Edgar	Private	Devons	India	
Guest, Albert	Private	Lancashires	France	Killed
Gilbert, Henry	Private	Devons	Home Service	
Hine, Ernest	Trooper	Devon Yeomanry	Palestine	
Hine, George	Gunner	RGA	France	
Hodges, William	Chaplain	HMHS Egypt	E.E.Force	
Hingston, Edwin	Artificer	Royal Navy	MS *Tiger*	
Hingston, Walter	Altificer	Royal Navy	Home Service	
Head, Albert	Gunner	Machine Gun Corps	France	
Inch, Thomas	Private	Devons	Egypt	
Jarred, Arthur	Sergeant	RAMC	France	Awarded M.M.
Jarred, Albert	Private	Staffords	France	Wounded
Jarred, Ernest	Stoker	Royal Navy	MS *Forth*	
Kennard, James	P.O.	Royal Navy	MS *Monnsey*	
Kennard, Walter	Stoker	Royal Navy	HMS *Tiger*	
Luscombe, Thomas	Private	Dorsets	France & Mesopotamia	
Luscombe, William	Private	Devons	France	
Luscombe, James	Private	Royal Marines		
Lethbridge, Frederick	Stoker	Royal Navy	MS *Saunders*	
Lakeman, Philip	Sergeant	RGA	France	
Lapthorne, King	Corpl	DCLI	France	Wounded twice

Name	Rank	Unit	Front	Remarks
Middlewick, James	Sapper	RE	France & Russia	
Mortimore, Walter T.	P.O.	Royal Navy	HMS *Goliath*	Killed at Dardanelles
Preston, George	Gunner	Mach. Gun Corps	France	
Preston, William H.		Royal Navy	HMS *Castor*	
Preston, Edwin	Private	AS Corps	France	Died on service
Preston, Arthur	Private	Devons	France	Wounded
Prowse, Charles	Stoker	Royal Navy	HMS *Tiger*	
Quick, Edwin	Private	Devons	France	Killed in action
Quick, Frank	A.B.	Royal Navy	HM Mine Sweeper	
Ryder, Thomas	Stoker	Royal Navy	HMS *Cassandra*	Killed by explosion
Ryder, Lionel	Gunner	RGA	France	
Rail, Frederick	Sergeant	Motor Transport	Home Service	
Shute, Stephanus	Sapper	RE	France	Killed in action
Stone, Redvers		Royal Navy	Home Service	
Squires, Daniel T.	P.O.	Royal Navy	HMS *Indefatigable*	Killed Jutland Battle
Skinner, Richard	Private	AV Corps	France	
Soper, Charles	Stoker	Royal Navy	HMS *King George*	
Soper, John	Stoker	Royal Navy	HMS *Watchman*	
Soper, Thomas	Stoker	Royal Navy	HMS *Lion*	
Soper, George	Stoker	Royal Navy	HMS *Warspite*	
Soper, Norman	Stoker	Royal Navy	HMS *Cordelia*	
Soper, William	Private	RAMC	France	
Soper, Henry	Gunner	RGA	France	
Sherrell, John	Corpl	Devon Yeomanry	Gallipoli, Palestine/France	Killed in action
Sherrell, William	Private	Dorsets	France	
Shepherd, Henry	Private	Devons	France	Killed in Action
Stear, James H.	Private	London Regt.	France	Wounded
Tapp, Frank	Cadet	RAForce		Died in Training
Tolchard, William	Private	Motor Transport	France	
Taylor, Walter	Private	Devons	France	Killed in Action
Taylor, Herbert (Albert)	Private	Devons	France	Killed in Action
Taylor, Percy	Private	Devons	France	Killed in Action
Taylor, William	Private	Devons	Home Service	
Winzer, John W.	Trooper	Devon Yeomanry	Gallipoli, Palestine/France	
Wakeley, Tom.W.G.	Private	Military Police	France	
Wise, Henry, Dacres	Capt.	18th Hussars	France	Awarded M.C.
Wise, Lancelot C.	Lieut.	Indian Cavalry	France & India	Died in India
Wise, Charles F.	Capt.	RFA	France	Wounded
Yabsley, Henry	Private	Labour Bn.	Home Service	

Men from Loddiswell Parish who served in
the 1914-18 and did not return were:

Harold Allin	Edwin Quick	Daniel Squires
Richard Brooking	Tom Ryder	Frank Tapp
William Eastley	Henry Shepherd	Albert Taylor
Albert Guest	John Sherrell	Walter Taylor
Walter Mortimore	Stephanus Shute	Percy Taylor
Edwin Preston	William Soper	Lancelot Wise

For the next 20 years Europe enjoyed an uncertain peace with conflicts throughout the 1920s and '30s. Russia came under the 'Iron Heel' and the ruthless dictatorship of Stalin. Britain was troubled by the Irish Rebellion and during the Uprising, Roger Grenville Peek, Captain of the 9th Lancers, was killed on duty on 23 March 1921. The British Empire, too, was seriously undermined by the spread of civil defiance or 'disobedience' in India.

Mussolini's Italian Forces invaded Abyssinia (Ethiopia) in October 1935 and from 1936 to 1939 civil disorder and then civil war gripped the Spanish Republic. This provided a convenient testing ground for the 'German War Machine' of tanks and aircraft. The alarming rise of Hitler's power and the establishment of the Nazi Regime through the 1930s made another war seem inevitable although every effort was made by the British Government to avert the turmoil that would follow. Those who did not return from the Second World War were:

George Brooking   Roger Peek
Leslie Brooking   George Skinner
John Dymond   Arthur Williams
Stanley Goss   Olivia Willing
John Martin   Herbert Yeoman

Ted Westlake, Clerk of the Parish Council, laying a wreath at the 1998 Remembrance Service.

Remembrance Day, 1998.

Jack Hine

Ronald
Birmingham

IN THEIR
SERVICE DAYS

Capt William
Peek

Ivan Pope

Cyril
Brooking

Owen Elliott

Dennis Sharland

Cyril Marshall

Walter Kernick

Walter Hine

Sheila Elliott

The men and women of the parish who served in the Second World War – as they are today (left) and as they were (above).
Left: Back (left to right): Cyril Marshall, Ivan Pope, Walter Kernick, Sheila Elliott, Owen Elliott; front: Cyril Brooking, Jack Hine, Walter Hine, Sir William Peek, Dennis Sharland; absent: Ronald Birmingham.

*Loddiswell men who served during the
Falklands War.
Left: Leading Seaman Paul Taylor.
Right: Able Seaman Marco Brimacombe.*

Prisoners of war meanwhile were: Horace Martin, Harold Skinner and John Martin.

Sapper John Martin (*pictured opposite page*) of Stanton Farm died from wounds received when taking part in the invasion of Normandy. Originally a gunner serving with the BEF in France in 1939, he was captured in Flanders during the retreat of May 1940. Escaping from his guards he wandered through the south for months, subsisting on the countryside he passed through. Twice he was recaptured and twice he succeeded in getting free – to arrive back in England at the end of 1940. For his services in France and for the great courage and resource which he displayed while detached from his unit he was awarded the DCM, a decoration which he received from King George VI.

Military deaths from Great Britain were about 265 000 with over 70 000 civilian deaths through the bombing of the towns and cities. Servicemen who married Loddiswell girls and spent their working lives in the parish include:

Ron Birmingham	Fred Riggall
Raymond Harvey	Ern Robinson
Fred Jackson	Bill Shepherd
Ron Lloyd	Dennis Sharland
Cyril Marshall	

In 1950 North Korea invaded South Korea and United Nations servicemen were called to arms. The war ended in July 1953 but it is not known whether any Loddiswell men were involved.

The British nation experienced grave concern in April 1982 when Argentina invaded the Falkland Islands. Britain was again thrust into another war, which, fortunately, was over by 14 June and, although tragedies occurred, the loss of life to Britain was not so great as that incurred during the wars of previous years. A total of 239 men

lost their lives. Paul Taylor and Marco Brimacombe both served in the Falklands War (*they are pictured opposite*).

In 1990 Iraq invaded Kuwait and Coalition Forces, from the USA, Britain and from 30 other countries, were deployed to drive back the Iraqi Forces. Gregory Kemsley served with the Royal Artillery there and Michael King served in the Merchant Navy.

Troubles in Northern Ireland still rumble on with loss of life through sectarian shootings and bomb attacks mainly affecting the civilian population.

*Loddiswell men who served during the Gulf War.
Above: Gregory Kemsley, Royal Artillery.
Inset: Michael King, Merchant Navy.*

REMINISCENCES AND REMEMBRANCE

Sandford Jeffery served in the Army during the war and was in Brussels in 1944. He was walking down a street on one occasion and his attention was drawn towards a soldier on the other side of the street who was carrying a bag slung over his shoulder. He bore his load just as a Loddiswell man would so Sandford crossed the street to speak to him. To his surprise it was indeed a Loddiswell man, Redford Watts, who lived not far from him at home. Until then he had no idea that Redford was in the Army.

John Horton and Walter Kernick met 53 years after the Second World War and discovered that they had been in fairly close proximity for three years in various places during and after the conflict. Walter was on his way to North Africa in a Navy mine-layer to join his night fighter squadron there. At Gibraltar he transferred to a US Coastguard Cutter and heading east at night came across a large troopship the *Strathallen* that had been torpedoed and was on fire. The majority of those on board were saved and taken into Oran, Algeria. John Horton was among the survivors and was in Army Intelligence in Algeria not far from the airfield where Walter's squadron was based. The following year, 1943, John crossed to Italy and Walter, then with the US Air Force, followed in 1944. Early in 1945 Walter joined a RAF squadron which was going to Burma and John was also transferred there. They both remained there to the end of the war and beyond. After the war John lived in Germany as part of the Military Government of Occupation and Walter lived there for years with the Air Force of Occupation. Neither was aware of this until meeting in 1998.

Above: Sapper Martin who died of wounds following the Normandy invasion of 1944.

Below: WAAF Serg. Joan Tyler (née Walke) presented to the Duchess of Gloucester at Mount Wise, Plymouth, July 1943.

List of Loddiswell Men and Women serving in the Armed Forces in the 1939-1940 World War

Bert Brown	Navy. Regular
John Brown	RAF Regular
Cyril Brooking	Navy, Submarines
George Brooking	Navy, Reg. and Res.
Glynn Brooking	RAF
Leslie Brooking	RAF
Wilf Burman	Army
George Bush	RAF Regular
Horace Camp	RAF
Clive Commons	Army
John Dymond	Army
Dennis Edgcombe	RAF Regiment
Fred Edgecombe	Army
Bill Edgecombe	Army
Bert Elliott	RAF
Owen Elliott	RAF
Percy Johns	Army
Jack Freeman	Army
Bill Gill	Army
Stanley Goss	Army
Ted Guest	Navy Regular
Jack Hawke	Army
Claude Hine	Army
Jack Hine	Army
Leslie Hine	Army
Leonard Hine	Army
Walter Hine	Army
Walter Hingston	Navy Regular
John (Bill) Horton	Army
Jack Hodge	Army
Sandford Jeffery	Army
Walter Kemick	RAF Regular
Bill Luscombe	Army
Harold Lethbridge	Army

Frank Mabin	Navy, Reg. and Res.
Johnny Marsh Senr.	RAF
John Martin	Army
Horace Martin	Army Reg.
William Peek	Army Tank Corp Reg
Roger Peek	Army Regular
Fred Parsliffe	Army
Ivan Pope	Army
Ted Quick	Army
Alf Ryder	Army
Chris Ryder	Army
Eric Ryder	Army
Raymond Ryder	Army
Jack Scoble	Air Sea Rescue
Harold Skinner	Army
George Skinner	Army
Bill Stone	Army
Arthur Taylor	Navy Reg. and Res.
Redford Watts	Army
Arthur Williams	Navy
George Williams	RAF Regiment
Harold Yalland	RAF Regular
Herbert Yeoman	Army

WOMEN'S ROYAL SERVICES

Sheila Elliott (née Taylor)	WRNS
Margary Jackson (née Brooking)	ATS
Pearl Jago (née Brooking)	WRNS
Winnifred Kirton (née Seldon)	WAAF
Alice Perry (née Hannaford)	ATS
Evelyn Pile	ATS
Cora Bradborn (née Ryder)	ATS
Joan Tyler (née Walke)	WAAF

Agnes Willing	Served as nurses throughout
Olivia Willing	the Plymouth bombing

IN DEFENCE OF OUR HOMES

In the Middle Ages it was the responsibility of each parish to provide men, armour and horses ready for military service. The parish armour was usually kept in the church and we can assume that Loddiswell was no different. Archers could cut quivers from the yew tree in the churchyard and perfect their skills at 'Loddiswell Butts' or 'Ham Butts' (both retain their names to this day).

A muster roll was kept and men with names on that roll could be called for service at any time. Beacons on the hilltops were ready and guarded by day and night so when an enemy was sighted they could be set alight. This was the signal for action. The Duke of Somerset's papers give instructions as to what was to be done:

All mustered are to repair to the Parish Church, there to arm themselves and to remain until they have directions from their Captains

The parish had to supply ten days' victuals or money for each soldier.

The 1569 muster roll mentioned that people who owned goods to the value of £10-20 had to provide equipment and men. Loddiswell provided ten archers, ten harquebusiers (handguns) and five pikemen.

A Rifle Volunteer Corps was formed at Kingsbridge in 1850 and men from surrounding villages joined in. There were frequent bazaars and concerts to raise money for this active body of men. They had a shooting range at Loddiswell near the river and entered shooting contests with success. When they went to camp at Mount Edgcumbe and other places they met with other rifle volunteers.

The threatening clouds of war loomed over us from 1937-39 and preparations began to be made for civil protection. An Air Raid Precautions Scheme (ARP) was instigated by the Rural District Council and Bert Bowden was appointed Air Raid Warden. Others were elected to form an Emergency Squad to prepare field kitchens, first aid and fire precautions. In September 1941 the Kingsbridge Joint Fire Brigade built a circular water storage tank in Well Street to supplement the hydrants in case of fire.

London was bombed in the spring of 1940 and children were evacuated to country areas for their safety. In June, 2500 evacuees from London came to the South Hams to live in volunteer homes and Loddiswell took a proportion of them. Lewis R. Sampson of Higher Yanston was the Billeting Officer for the area who found accommodation for them. Some returned to their homes, or what remained of them when the heavy bombing ceased. The second wave of evacuees arose out of the horror and devastation caused by the arrival of VI and V2 bombs towards the end of the war. Ruth Hyne was one of these and she tells of how she was sent by train straight from Paddington to Kingsbridge and from there by coach to Loddiswell accompanied by the school teachers, Miss Common, Miss Michell and Miss Todd. Ruth stayed with Mr and Mrs Bert Bowden, the shoe repairer at No.1. The Bank.

The Women's Voluntary Service (WVS) formed in 1938 was an amalgamation of already existing bodies who gave their services in hospitals, assisted victims of air-raids, and cared for and helped evacuees in transit. They also helped with the clerical work involved with the annual distribution of ration books. Petrol coupons were allocated and mileage allowances were made for the few WVS members who had cars under the Volunteer Car Pool.

The Hon. Mrs Joan Peek was the Rural Area Organiser and other WVS members from Loddiswell were Ethel Hine, Clara Horton, Eva Kernick and Dorothy Taylor. Food and clothing ration books were collected from the Rural Food Office at the Manor House and from the Urban Council Office, Kingsbridge. In 1943 both offices were amalgamated and housed in No.2 Vine Terrace. The WVS distributed the Loddiswell ration books at the Reading Room (Corner Cottage).

Food rationing came into operation in January 1940 and continued until 1954, some commodities – tea, sugar and shell eggs – being rationed until 1953, and butter, cheese and meat until the following year. As the allowances of essential foods were so minimal, the basic wartime food relied principally on potatoes and home-grown wheat. Potatoes were not only used in savoury dishes but incorporated in cakes and

Jean Baker, Women's Land Army (1942-48).

The Hon. Mrs Joan Peek (far left), WVS Rural Area Organiser, 1943.

pastries. Bread was not rationed during the war but afterwards (1946-48) due to the severe post-war shortages. Butter, margarine, meats, tea, sugar and dried eggs were all rationed by coupons in buff ration books; some tinned foods, dried lentils, peas, rice and cereals were supplied on a points allocation for individual choice if the products were available. Doctors gave expectant mothers certificates to be taken to the Food Office where they were issued green ration books in place of the normal buff ones. It entitled them to an extra half ration of meat, an extra egg, an extra pint of milk, some vitamins A and D and extra clothing coupons. When the baby was born the ration book became the child's. Children from 5 to 16 years were issued with blue books which entitled them to an extra half pint of milk a day. Cod liver oil, orange juice, rosehip syrup and national dried milk were issued as a supplement to young children.

White bread was discontinued throughout the war and was replaced by the 'National Loaf' which was made by using all the grain. It was said that although the British nation became lean they were never healthier. The Reading Room became a 'field kitchen' where local residents could take their surplus fruit to be preserved. Kilner jars were supplied for bottling fruit and a limited supply of sugar was allocated for this and for jam making. A large boiler was installed for the purpose.

Each man, woman and child was allocated 66 clothing coupons. When an occasional village wedding took place, relatives, friends and neighbours would rally round to provide coupons for the bride's trousseau. A short dress and jacket would need 22 coupons, shoes 5, two nightdresses 12, four sets of underwear 12, two pairs of stockings 4, gloves 2 and a cardigan or blouse 5.

In the South Hams the local WVS were called in November 1943 to help evacuate Slapton and the surrounding villages as the area was to be used

Left: Lewis R. Sampson, Billetting Officer, 1940-44. Right: Herbert (Bert) Bowden, Air Raid Warden 1939-45.

as a training ground before the invasion of Normandy on D Day, 6 June 1944.

Towards the end of the First World War the need for men to support the Armed Forces was so great that women were recruited to serve on the land. The Women's Land Army was formed in 1917 and continued until 1920. With the outbreak of war in 1939, the need for home-grown food was of paramount importance and it was once again revived under the War Agricultural Committee. The local organiser for the South Hams was Mrs Gladys Conran of Blackwell Parks.

Many of the girls who joined were billeted in hostels and were taken each day by lorry to farms to do routine work or seasonal planting and harvesting. The hostel serving the South Hams was at Charleton Court, near Kingsbridge. Jean Baker served in the army from 1942-48 and 'lived in' at Lukesland Farm. She has lived in the parish ever since her marriage to Russell Baker. Jean Wood joined as a teenager from Kent and was billeted in a hostel at Chagford and then Buckfastleigh. She came to live in Loddiswell in 1948, after her marriage. Sheila Balkwill and Helen Robins, former Land Army Girls, have in more recent years made their homes here.

Wartime wedding of Dorothy Yabsley and Walter Gardner. Left to right: Zoe Brock, Mabel Goss, Mrs Hendy, ?, Louise Hambley, Frances Bird, Mrs M. Pope, Queenie Hine, ?, Mr Sherriff (Totnes), ?, Walter Gardner, ?, Dorothy Yabsley, ?, Pat Yabsley, Nancy Yabsley, Selina Yabsley (bride's mother), Violet Mabin, Robert Yabsley, Eva Kernick, Bill Yabsley (bride's father), Dawn Mabin (little girl in front).

LODDISWELL HOME GUARD

The evacuation from Dunkirk between 27 May and 4 June 1940 raised the fear of an invasion or at least the dropping of spies, paratroopers or saboteurs into the countryside. The Local Defence Volunteers (LDV) was formed and their first operation was to look out for any enemy activity at night from a post at the reservoir on Blackdown. The unit was soon renamed the 'Home Guard' and the platoon was rapidly trained in the use and maintenance of military equipment. Rifle practice was held regularly at Morleigh or Yanston, and live grenades were thrown on Burgh Island. Dr Cowper briefed the platoon in first aid at the Drill Hall in Modbury and survival in the presence of mustard gas at Aveton Gifford.

Manoeuvres and all-night exercises prepared the men for mock battles against the Commandos, and on one occasion when Stanley Hine, a Loddiswell Home Guardsman, was being taken prisoner, a Loddiswell lady intercepted and forced the Commando to release him.

Enemy raids began during the summer of 1940, intensifying the following spring when Plymouth was bombed. On the two nights of 20 and 21 March, £100 million worth of damage was done to 20 000 properties and 336 people were killed.

Two high explosive bombs (HE) were dropped in Court House fields on 7 May 1941 and houses in the Courtledge area were badly shaken. Fortunately the blast was directed beyond the village towards Reveton Farm, a mile away where the front door was blown open. Even so, seven of the Loddiswell Church windows were badly damaged.

The risk of enemy invasion seemed imminent in 1942 and the Home Guard Platoons were briefed in tactics aimed at impeding and delaying any enemy force. Loddiswell New Bridge was ready to be covered by machine gun fire from two positions at any time with support from a flame trap and anti-tank grenades.

Loddiswell Home Guard Platoon, 1943
(Left to right) back row: Cyril Brooking, Reg Cole, Roy Adams, Harold Cole, Vic Hallett, John Paynter,
John Pedrick;
3rd row: John Netting, Tom Luscombe, Fred Hine, Bill Hine, Dick Perring, Bill Brooking, Tom Brooking,
Tom Rundle, Frank Lilley;
2nd row: Alfred Ball, Herbert Harvey, Ian Earle, Harris Lethbridge, Chris Pedrick, Theo Willing, Fred Perring,
Rich Rogers, Leslie Sampson;
front row: L/Cpl Reg Sampson, Cpl George Stephens, Cpl Percy Baker, Sub/Lt. Tom Hannah, Lt. Sidney Scoble,
Sgt Lionel Ryder, Harry Stacey, Jim Hine, Tom Skinner;
Members of the Home Guard who were attending a course at Kingsbridge and not in the photograph:
Wally Tarr, Herman Hosking, Jack Caunter, Bill Seldon, Harry Withers.

Atwill Walke on pony, cousin of Walter Walke of Hazelwood and his daughter Audrey with the harvest rabbits, 1928.

Farm workers taking a welcome break.

Chapter 14: Farming 1850-2000

In 1850 the *White's Directory* of Devon listed 29 farms in Loddiswell Parish, which stretched from Hazelwood in the north to Hatch in the south. The number of farmers remained fairly static throughout the 19th century right up to the Second World War and this was probably because horse and man were the main sources of power. Farming reached highs and lows of profitability throughout this period. From 1815 to 1830 farmers took a severe shock with the fall of agricultural prices when many lost their capital and were forced to become 'operatives to others'. This widespread ruin caused great distress to landlords and tenants alike and all those immediately dependent upon them.

From 1830 the farming communities assumed a more stable condition as landlords lowered rents and tenants were gradually able to recover. British farming in the 1850s and '60s attained as high a level of efficiency and intensiveness as found anywhere in the world. Landlords increased rents again but despite this farmers were still able to make large profits. It was during this prosperous period that landlords started to erect large farm buildings and to improve farmhouses, an example of this being where the huge range of buildings was erected in the 1870s at Stanton Farm

The weather in 1879 was disastrously wet and cold and signalled the end of the boom years. In North America the reaper and later the string- or self-binder had been invented, allowing the acreage of wheat to be vastly increased. During this period the North Americans were building a network of railways which enabled the wheat to be transported the long distances to the ports. Wheat flooded into the UK depressing the market to unprecedented low prices of about 5 shillings per cwt. Frozen meat soon began to come into the country from overseas and that, too, had a detrimental effect on British agriculture generally.

The depression was not, however, felt so acutely in Devon and Cornwall where holdings were smaller and the fields were enclosed. The financial crisis halted any expansion or improvement of buildings and the number of farm workers declined generally, although there was, at the same time, an expansion of dairy and pig production. There was a general deterioration in land husbandry especially in poorer pastures where drainage and cultivation were neglected. An example of this is in Andrew's Wood (Stanton Moor) where the small fields and enclosures were left for Mother Nature to take her course and by 1950 it was almost impossible to walk through the scrub trees, thorns, brambles and bracken. Capt. W.A.B. Conran, whose cattle often grazed there, was often unable to find them for many days and this caused him grave concern.

The outbreak of the First World War in 1914 brought a renewed stability in farming but this was short lived with the onset of the great depression in 1929. Until then the labour requirement on a farm was high and all cultivation relied on horse power. On an average farm the general calculation was one horse for every 25 acres, although this depended of course on the type of farming and the contours of the land.

During this period there was a similarity between farms, each with ten to fifteen cows, three or four sows and litters, thirty to forty ewes and the inevitable hens, ducks and geese that wandered around the farmyard. A horseman was classified as the head farm worker and was in charge of his team of horses, which were fed and groomed before he took breakfast at 7.30am He had to be ready to start ploughing at 8am, in order to plough the expected one acre a day. On large arable farms, especially the large estate farms, workmen's cottages were included in the tenancy, but on smaller farms the workers came from the village or young men lived in at the farmhouse. Most farmers' wives employed a girl who also lived in or came from the local village to help with the work. The chores were very heavy when water had to be pumped and carried for all domestic use. Needless to say, if the farmhouse had live-in labour, wash-day was a major operation.

The dairy work was quite considerable as the milk was separated, the cream scalded and made into butter for the weekly pannier market at the nearest town. This was the big event of the week with the preparation, not only of the butter and cream, but also of eggs, chickens, rabbits and sometimes hogs-pudding made on the farm. It

Stanton Barns built in the prosperous farming era in 1870 for a farm of 300 acres.

C.F. Osmond's 1875 accounts of cattle and sheep at Reveton Farm.

was a case of survival rather than a way of life, just providing a meagre living for the farmer and his family. Cattle were reared and sold in order to pay the rent and many farmers' wives resorted to taking in summer visitors to supplement their livings. Stanton and part of Woolston farms were unoccupied during 1938 and 1939. Weeds grew, hedges became overgrown and rabbits bred and multiplied at an alarming rate.

The outbreak of the Second World War in 1939 forced a major change in the whole of British agriculture. The main emphasis was then placed on the production of essential foods; cereals, potatoes, sugar-beet, milk and vegetables. The War Agriculture Committees were formed with officials and representative farmers in each county overseeing and monitoring production. Each farmer was required to plough about two-thirds of their land, bringing some of their prime grazing into arable production. The urgent need for food was so acute that even ancient sites such as the Blackdown Rings were ploughed for cereal and potato production.

The drive for maximum food production continued for several years after the war due to the wartime devastation in Europe. The Government pledged that the prosperity of farming must never again be allowed to decline. It is ironic, that as we approach the 21st century, farming profits have taken a serious downturn.

Farming in the 1960's and '70s reached the highest production and profitability of the century as a result of new technology, mechanisation and Government support. Farmers were unaware of the looming catastrophe which would soon hit all dairy and beef herds in the country. In 1986 cows were diagnosed with the brain disorder BSE (Spongiform Encephalopathy), thought, by some, to be caused by feeding concentrated cattle nuts containing meat and bone meal.

The ban on all British beef by European and other nations caused prices to collapse. Drastic measures were taken and all cattle over two-and-a-half years old were not allowed to enter the human food chain. Most British households considered the risk of eating beef to be minimal so the home market gradually became more confident. However, the meat industry relies on the export market and this needed to be re-established to provide an outlet for British beef. As EU and Government support for all agricultural products has lessened, farmers have been compelled to take stringent cost-saving measures in order to survive.

Tunley Farm House, c.1895. The property is recorded as 'Tonleigh' in 1330 and 'Townleigh' in 1660 (i.e. near a 'tun' or village).

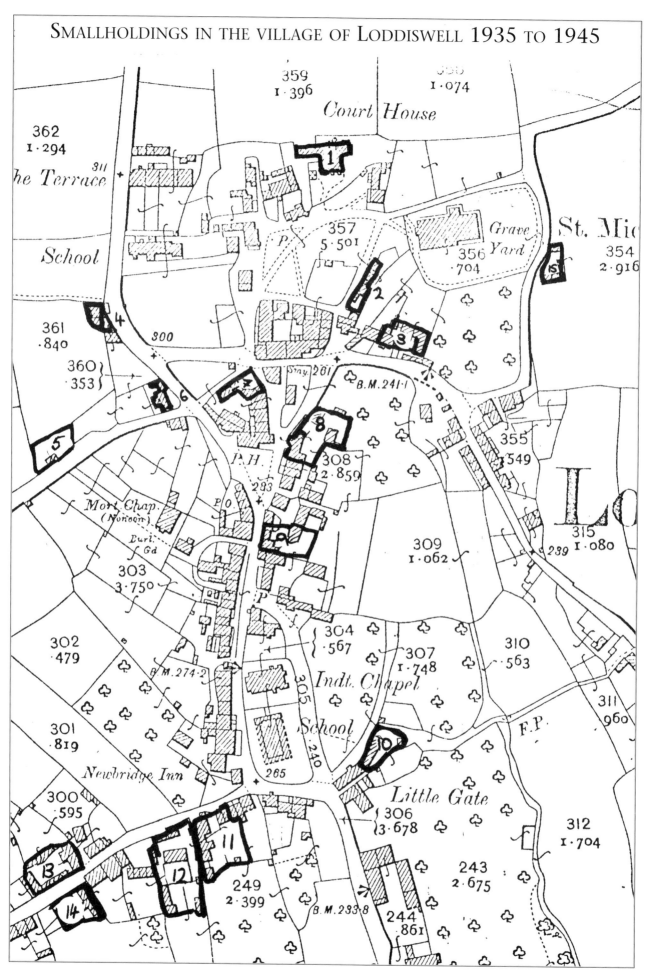

SMALLHOLDINGS IN THE VILLAGE OF LODDISWELL 1935 TO 1945

SMALL DAIRY UNITS TO 1940

Until almost the middle of the 20th century rural communities were largely self sufficient as many families had a small-holding or allotment and grew their own vegetables. Household waste was fed to a pig in a sty near the back door and a few hens kept the family supplied with eggs.

Within the village of Loddiswell there were 15 small dairy units of two or three cows although a couple of homesteads, particularly at Storridge and Wyselands, kept several more. Neighbours bought the surplus milk and eggs, and on Sundays, would indulge in the luxury of a dish of separated or clotted cream.

Above: A common sight up until the 1960s when cows returned to the shippen in the village for milking. Heather Harding bringing in her father's herd at Wyselands, 1960.

Below: Wally Tarr milking the house cow at Inner Weeke.

KEY TO MAP OPPOSITE

1. William Elliott at Park and Court House.
2. Eddie Pratt and later Dick Lethbridge at Storridge.
3. Jimmy and Alice Yalland at Pointridge.
4. Ned Yalland at Stile Cottage.
5. Jim Middlewick and later Arthur ('Buck') Taylor at Veroak Park (Oakwood Park).
6. John Yalland at Silveridge.
7. Percy Stephens at Little Reads.
8. Bob Yabsley and later Cyril Harding at Wyselands.
9. John Sandover at Providence Place.
10. Redford Watts and later Theo Willing at Little Gate.
11. Tom Rundle at Cross Farm.
12. Tom Squires, George and Sid Brooking and Wilfred Jane at Greystones.
13. Harry Yabsley at Treeby's (Mead Court).
14. Trowbridge Horton at Vine House.
15. Bert Walke at Station Road.

113

DIVERSIFICATION

Land use and housing during the 20th century has been transformed by mechanisation and the availability of cars for rural transport. Some of the large aristocratic houses have been converted into hotels or self-catering homes. Woolston House and stables were converted in the 1970s to eight self-catering apartments, then later to a hotel and back again to self-catering. The walled garden which supplied fruit and vegetables for the occupants of the house in the early part of the century was converted into tennis courts and a heated swimming pool.

Hazelwood House was sold away from the Hazelwood Estate and now provides accommodation for guests with a wide range of interests in music and the arts. It is a place of extraordinary peace and beauty in the heart of the South Devonshire countryside. The house is set in 67 acres of woodland, meadows, river bank and orchards which are ideal for walking, painting or simply relaxing. Jane Bowman's watercolour weekends are inspiring and explore the depth and versatility of watercolour, and concerts, cultural events and courses take place at Hazelwood throughout the year. Events in the late 1990s have ranged from the Medici String Quartet and Lindisfarne in Concert, to Manray and a mixture of latin and jazz.

Some farmhouses have converted a part of their house and outbuildings to self-catering and others to en-suite facilities for bed and breakfast.

Visitors have been welcomed at Crannacombe, Aveton, Blackwell Parks, Great Gate, Hatch, Pointridge, Reads, Reveton, Tunley and Yanston.

Andrew's Wood was leased and in 1965 was given to the Devon Trust for Nature Conservation by Col. Walker of Woolston House. It was classified as a Site of Special Scientific Interest under the Wildlife and Countryside Act 1981. One of the fields near Andrew's Wood has been excavated, forming two large lakes, covering approximately three and seven acres, for private carp fishing.

Loddiswell Vineyard planted a small plot of vines for wine making in 1972 and after a period of experimentation the main vineyard was planted in 1977. The first four acres were increased to ten by 1980, and the vineyard benefited from good weather in 1982, 1983 and 1984 (when production increased to 18 tons, peaking in 1990 when 40 000 bottles were produced). The wines were made at the vineyard and sold to the visiting public and local shops and hotels until 1996 when Reg and Betty Sampson retired.

Steve and Shirley Bradley began producing cider and apple juice at Crannacombe in 1996 under the name of 'Heron Valley'. Crannacombe means Cranescombe, literally 'Valley of the Herons'. Old varieties of cider apples from their own orchards and from other small family farms are traditionally used for cider making. A blend of varieties are pressed for a standard apple juice and a rather sweeter, organic juice is also made and has become very popular. After many years in the business of cider making Steve has installed a modern crusher and hydraulic press which is used during the processing period from September to Christmas. After bottling, the product is sold to public houses, shops and hotels throughout the South West.

Top: Steve Bradley, the proprietor of Heron Valley Devon Cider, checking a bottle, 1998.

Left: The grape pickers at Loddiswell Vineyard, 1985: Ann Janes, Sally Henderson, Sue Sweeney, Diane Hollett, Sue Weston, Fred Diamond, Helen Reeve, Janet Wellens, Phil Hayhurst, Marcia Dutton.

Loddiswell Vineyard

Left: Neil Hockin and Andrew Sampson summer pruning.

Above: Reg Sampson filtering wine, 1990.
Left: Julie Bennett bottle filling apple juice, 1998.
Below: Filling the grape trailer.

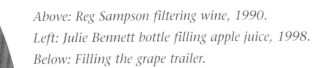

Ham Farm

Below: The kitchen hearth at Ham Farm, 1914.

Alfred Hingston Senr and daughter Louie returning to the farm in the trap, 1914.

Left: Mrs Hingston (Michael and Jane Rose's great-grandmother) and daughters Louie and Ethel feeding the flock of chickens, turkeys and ducks, 1914.

Below: Alfred Hingston Senr with his flock, 1914.

LANDLORD/TENANT AND OWNER/OCCUPIER SYSTEMS

In a survey of Loddiswell in 1602/3 there is a reference to a lease of Halswood (Hazelwood) of some 70 acres to Simon Phillipps for 99 years at a rent of 10s.1d. quarterly. The following extract is taken from it:

On the death of the tenant's Sons or a surrender of the lease the land will be vacated and the landlord will claim 'Sute to the courte, and a best beast or 40/- at the choice of the lord... in the name of a heriott' [a fine due to the Lord of the Manor on the death of a tenant] and to have sufficient housebott [tenants' right to wood to repair his house] and haybott, hedgbott [to repair hedges], firebott [firewood] and ploughbott [to repair the wooden ox ploughs], frith [brushwood] and stacke without delay doing no waste.

A lease of Coombe Farm to John Came (great-grandfather of John Came, The Terrace) for 14 years from 1837 states that the tenant shall be permitted to grow arable crops for three years in any seven years on the arable land. In the first of these three years:

... the tenant shall spread 12 hogsheads [casks of 52 gallons] of good well burnt stone lime per acre. In the last year the land shall be seeded out with 10 lbs good new clover and 1 peck [2 gallons] of eaver with 6 hogshead of burnt time.

A century later in the 1920s and '30s clauses in the tenancy agreements required the tenant:

To farm, cultivate, manure and manage the farm in a good and husbandlike manner according to the most approved methods of husbandry in the district so as to keep the whole at all times in good heart and condition and not to allow any part to become impoverished by exhausting crops or otherwise.

To farm the arable land on the four course system, that is to say, to have as nearly as the sizes of the fields will admit, one fourth in turnips or mangolds, one fourth in barley or oats sown with clover or other artificial grass seed, one fourth in clover or grass sown in the previous year and the remaining fourth in wheat.

It had long been recognised by the farming fraternity that more than two 'white straw' crops could impoverish the soil but during the second half of the 20th century the theories of plant management and nutritional requirements have been more clearly understood and applied. The

Above: George Farley Shepherd with his son, George Edmund, at Higher Yanston, 1897.

Left: Russell Baker's family of Bakers and Nettings at Heathfield Barton, 1928.
Left to right: Dorothy Netting, Mary Netting, Daisy Baker, Beatrice Baker (Gran), Mary Baker, ?, Dorothy Baker, Carrie Netting (Mother), Amy Netting (Gran), child in front, Amy Netting.

The Hosking Family

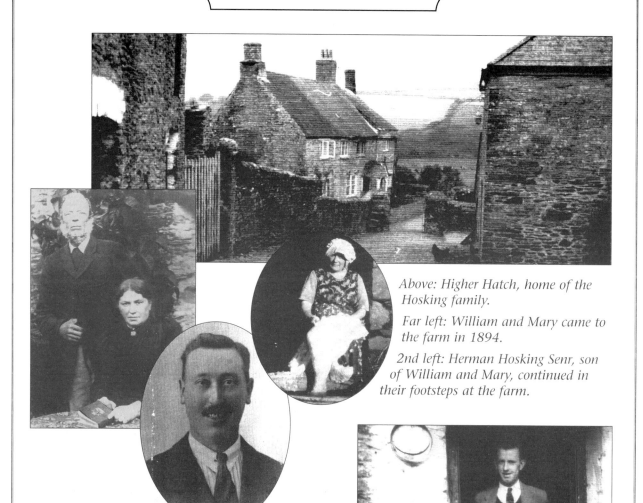

Above: Higher Hatch, home of the Hosking family.

Far left: William and Mary came to the farm in 1894.

2nd left: Herman Hosking Senr, son of William and Mary, continued in their footsteps at the farm.

Above centre: Jennifer Hosking's grandmother plucking the Christmas goose, 1928.

Above: In 1943 Higher Hatch was purchased for Herman Hosking Junr.

Far left: Great-grandson John has farmed there since 1970 when his father died.

Left: Great, great-grandson Peter now helps his father on the farm.

growing of oil seed rape, linseed, sunflowers, sugarbeet and potatoes has increased the opportunity of using alternative 'break crops'.

In 1940 some farms were owner-occupied and others tenanted, there being 11 of the former and 18 of the latter in Loddiswell Parish at that time. The Woolston estate encompassed Wigford, Coombe, Woolston, Stanton, Blackwell Parks, Wyselands, New Barn and several small fields around the village, amounting to just over 1000 acres and all these farms were tenanted. During the early 1940s nearly all the farms of this estate were sold and some were bought by the owners of the Hazelwood estate. They continued to increase their lands from other owners at the northern end of the parish by purchasing Heathfield Barton and Lower Hazelwood.

Tenanted farms changed hands quite frequently up to this period as farmers stayed for a few years before moving on to a better farm or a more generous landlord. The owner-occupied farmers tried to build and improve their farms for themselves and for the benefit of the next generation. In Loddiswell the Hosking family have lived at Hatch for over 100 years and are still there. This is also the case at Higher and Lower Yanston where

Michael Rose's great-grandfather started in 1897. Laskey Elliott's great-grandfather, James Moore, began farming at Knap Mill in 1905. Bertram Tarr moved into Outer (Lower) Weeke in 1935 and his son Wallace took over in 1947 and lives at Inner (Higher) Weeke. Jack Joint, Harold's father, came to Inner Weeke from Morleigh in 1919 and moved to Wigford in 1921. Harold continued farming there until he and May retired to Elmwood Park in 1978. William Lethbridge, Harold's father, farmed Coombe in the 1930s and the family remained there until 1990.

Higher Hazelwood was occupied by the Baker Family from 1839 to 1948. John Walke came to Lower Hazelwood as a tenant in 1869, his son John Stephen Walke bought the farm in 1919 and his family remained there until 1955. George Harvey became the owner-occupier of Tunley in 1929 followed by his son Herbert and the farm is now run by his grandson Paul Harvey. Reg Sampson's father moved to Tunley in 1923 and on to Higher Yanston in 1928 with the family moving 12 years later to Woolston Farm where John now farms. Arthur Rogers was married in 1939 and began farming at Aveton, where his son Michael still farms.

FARM MECHANISATION

Machines on the farm developed slowly through the years. For decades corn was cut with a scythe or sickle which required skill to cut the swathe evenly and close to the ground. A skilled reaper could mow up to two acres a day and it was not until after the 1850s that the horse-drawn reapers began to appear. A note in the *Kingsbridge Gazette* in 1859 reported:

Mr Cutmore has bought a new reaping machine which can reap, with two horses and one man, one acre an hour. Many farmers are interested in this wonderful machine.

The Howard and Hornsby reapers were substantially constructed and left the crop to be tied by hand.

At the turn of the century the reaper/binder began to take over thus eliminating the labour of binding the sheaves. Six or eight sheaves were stooked together to dry for a week before carting to the rickyard where they were stacked ready for threshing during the winter months.

Threshing days were red letter days. The steam traction engine and thresher moved around the parish from farm to farm. Coal and water were supplied by the farmer and nine or ten men were required to help. Neighbours from the

adjoining farms were expected to be ready to start before 8.30am. A couple of days threshing on one's own farm would mean eight or ten days helping neighbours in return. Sheaves were pitched from the rick on to the thresher where a man cut the sheaf

New Holland 8060 Combine-harvester at Woolston Farm, 1994.

ties and fed them into the drum. Humphrey Phelps in the *Countryman* writes:

The drum was like an insatiable monster gobbling sheaves as fast as we could feed it. It belched out dust, poured out corn at one end, straw at the other and cavings, or doust, beneath it. If an uncut sheaf fell into it, its guts rumbled. Hour after hour it ruled us; we were its slaves.

The straw tumbled onto an elevator to be carried to a rick or into a trusser which automatically tied the straw into large bundles. The most unpleasant job was clearing the chaff from under the machine which was usually the boy's job. On threshing days there was a plentiful supply of

Farm Machines Old and New

Top: Threshing at Higher Yanston, 1936.

Above: A self-binder cutting wheat.

Above: Cyril Harding with Bert Tarr on a load of bales, 1954.

Right: Cutting grass with a disc mower at Woolston Farm, 1979.

Farm Machines Old and New

Top: Loading silage with the forage harvester, 1979.

Above: Matbra loading round straw bales, 1998.

Above right: Paul Harvey milking in his 16-stall Herringbone parlour, 1999.

Right: Round straw bales in transit, 1998.

cider to quench their thirst, keeping everyone cheerful and encouraging their return another day.

In 1938 a few small combine-harvesters were to be seen on Salisbury Plain. They were hauled along by crawler tractors but few appeared in Devon until after the Second World War. Some were pulled by tractors but self-propelled combines soon started up in Loddiswell, usually owned by a contractor. They were bagging models that filled the two-cwt, West-of-England sacks and dropped them onto the ground. It was a laborious task collecting them and taking them to the store, and farmers were glad when the tanker combines replaced them. Grain would be discharged into a trailer running alongside and transported in bulk to the drier.

In the West Country the moisture content of the grain was often too high for storage so various types of grain driers were installed. The earlier combines were able to harvest about 10 acres a day but by the 1990s the much larger machines could cover four times that area.

Hay making was difficult in the South West because of the damp climate and with the invention of the tractor hydraulic lift and the Paterson buckrake, silage became popular. The buckrake was not very suitable for hauling grass from the outlying fields and during the 1950s was gradually replaced by the direct-cut forage harvester which blew the lacerated crop directly into a trailer towed behind or running alongside.

The silage was stored in clamps on a concrete base and the cows or cattle were allowed to feed from the clamp face. In order to keep the feeding face straight they were controlled by an electric fence.

As concentrated feed and grain became more costly a greater emphasis was placed on the quality of the grassland crops. To reduce the moisture content the grass was cut and left to wilt for a few days before being picked up with a single- or double-chop, forage harvester. The silage, having been chopped to short lengths, was more readily accessible for the cows and cattle. During the 1980s and '90s the whole system has been virtually replaced by the use of the round baler. The silage is pressed into round bales of a quarter to a third of a ton in weight, wrapped in polythene and handled by a tractor or self-propelled loader.

Many of the old stone barns are unsuitable for storing crops with this equipment and have become redundant. Their unique characteristics can often be retained by their conversion to residential units with the permission of the Local Planning Authority.

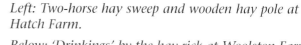

Left: Two-horse hay sweep and wooden hay pole at Hatch Farm.

Below: 'Drinkings' by the hay rick at Woolston Farm, 1947. Left to right: POW, Hermann Capito (POW), Frank Lilley, Reg Sampson, Sybil Sampson, Lewis Reg Sampson.

Chapter 15: The River Avon, Mills and Malt Houses

The River Avon has sustained a strong human population in the parish over the centuries, not only with the five miles of river which teemed with salmon and brown trout, but also with the abundantly supplied wells and streams and the coppices and woods which offered good hunting and fuel. Salmon from the river were so plentiful that they were not classified as a luxury. Servants who lived in and apprentices employed on the large estates several centuries ago often had a clause in their contracts stipulating that salmon should not be served to them more that three times a week, and some London apprentices also expressed this wish.

This was in stark contrast to the diet of the poor in Pagan times. The Celts held the sea in religious awe and the eating of fish was forbidden. Seas around our coast were teeming with fish and our rivers full of salmon and brown trout. By the 11th century, Catholicism was well established in Britain and the vast stocks of fish began to be exploited.

The decline in salmon stocks has frequently been attributed to high levels of pollution but extensive fishing, often with nets up to 20 miles long in the North Atlantic and the west of the British Isles, and trawlers fishing on the east side and up into Greenland and Icelandic waters decimated the migrating salmon population. In order to prevent the raiding of these fish stocks the North Atlantic Salmon Trust was formed in 1988 to buy fishing quotas from the Danes, Greenlanders, Icelanders and from the Faeroe Islands. Funds have been raised by private individuals, companies and members of the fishing associations by way of an annual levy of £2 per head for the fund.

Until the First World War the river was controlled by the owners of the adjoining lands. The fishing then on the Rivers Avon and Erme was controlled by a Board of Conservators who appointed a water bailiff to be responsible for catching poachers, and checking the fishing permits of anglers on the river.   They were Capt. W.G. Peek and Mr Cornish-Bowden who appointed Alfred Martin of Crannacombe as the last water bailiff under the control of the Conservators. By 1960 many sections of the river were controlled by the River Board and their bailiff in the 1960s was Tom Fowler. When the Avon Fisheries Association was formed it controlled 14 miles of river, the fishing rights of which were owned by them or rented from riparian owners and let to their 55 members. In 1998 two river wardens were employed to safeguard their interest on the Rivers Dart, Avon and Erme. Jim Coombes started fishing on the Avon in 1962 and in 1978 became Secretary and Treasurer of the Association. His untiring enthusiasm continues to the present time.

When the river was controlled by the local water bailiff the thrill and excitement of poaching was a challenge to the many locals who took out salmon under the cover of darkness. The salmon were poached with a four- or seven-prong spear on a long shaft, or snared in a wire loop dangled on the end of a stick; the loop was hitched over its tail or head and quickly pulled up.

Salmon poaching was commonplace on the river, and estate owners expected the water bailiffs to protect their interests. Stories of poaching exploits have been passed down through the generations. As young men Percy and Lionel Ryder, Frank Quick and Sid Hine were leaning innocently over Avon Bridge observing the salmon working upstream when the water bailiff of Bedlime appeared and said 'You won't catch nort here. You better go up above Silveridge.' This was his territory where he could apprehend them for loitering with intent.

The largest salmon poached was 41lbs, taken near Gara Bridge in 1935 by Alf Heath. The bailiff at that time was Charlie Stabbs who knew of the salmon and warned Alf not to take it. Alf waited until he knew the bailiff was safely out of the district and he and his brother Bill set out to catch it. Alf waited hanging on a tree branch and as it swam under him, speared it. They sold it to a local farmer for 6d. per pound. Sergeant Hawkins, a retired police officer from South Brent became the bailiff after Charlie Stabbs retired.   He could

Alf Ball, rabbit trapper, with his panniered donkey.

*Les Brimacombe demonstrates the poacher's art with his father-in-law's
copper snare, 1998.*

occasionally be more tolerant to the local poachers and would sometimes say to them 'I'm off to Morleigh for a drink', leaving the coast clear for a couple of hours.

Quite large salmon were often caught during the 1920s and '30s and Walter Kernick recalls on one occasion in 1934 when he and Pascoe Bush were walking up by the river at Silveridge where they found a huge salmon lying in shallow water which had recently been killed. Its head was damaged by teeth marks probably inflicted by an otter. They carried it home and it was divided between the neighbours.

The saying 'Trapper by trade, poacher by nature' applied to the many trappers bordering the River Avon. Bill Pullyblank was a gifted local orator and could entertain tirelessly with his tales of rabbit trapping and poaching. He could elude the most astute bailiff and although his cottage at Gara Bridge was on the other side of the road, his activities extended well into Loddiswell Parish. When anyone encroached on 'his patch' he could convincingly relate stories of the 'headless horseman' who roamed the woods and river banks after dark.

In the past it was said a true Loddiswell man always carried a bag on his back. Alf Ball was a rabbit trapper in Loddiswell Parish until the 1950s when the scourge of myxomatosis cleared most of the rabbit population. During his working life he used about 300 traps which he moved on every three or four days covering the parish. He relied on his donkey to carry them and each morning collected the rabbits – often over 100 in a single night. He was regularly seen taking them to Loddiswell Station or even taking them himself on his heavy ex-Post Office bicycle to a dealer in Plymouth. Alf Ball was very skilled at catching rabbits and perhaps the odd salmon if the opportunity arose. He eventually took out a fishing licence and this enabled him to dispose of his fish legally. The local poachers soon took advantage of this and would drop their illicit catches inside his front door much to the annoyance of his wife.

It was not only illegal to catch fish from the river without a licence at this time for game was also protected and belonged to the estate owners. While trapping rabbits it was inevitable that the occasional fox, badger or pheasant would be caught. One evening Alf was returning home carrying a pheasant in his bag when he met a friend who had 60 mackerel after a day's sea fishing. He offered the fish to Alf for 6d., who piled them into his bag on top of the pheasant. As he neared Loddiswell he was accosted by the local Police Constable who demanded to know what he was carrying. Alf quickly found the pheasant's leg through the bag and, firmly catching hold of it, tossed the bag upside down scattering the

Herbert George Walke (Butcher) fishing at the mouth of the Avon in 1967.

mackerel on the grass. 'There,' he said, 'only fish and now you can help me pick them up again'.

The Walke Brothers of Lower Hazelwood had land adjoining the river and Bert could take out the odd salmon with impeccable skill. Bathroom facilities did not exist in farmhouses so after a tiring summer's day shearing sweaty and troublesome sheep the boys and the farm worker set off to the river for a good wash. Charlie Freeman was always reluctant to allow the water above his knees so the boys eventually pushed him into an open-ended barrel and manoeuvred it out into mid stream with poles and pushed him to and fro until the barrel tipped over. Charlie had a long, wispy moustache and as his head appeared above the ripples his moustache drooped down reminiscent of a South Sea walrus.

The river has seen many ecological changes over the past decades. A thriving fish population which supported otters, kingfishers, dippers and herons went into decline in the 1970s and '80s when mink were a great scourge. They decimated the resident and migratory population of the river and its banks, but in the 1990s the trend has shown signs of being reversed as the mink are in decline, controlled now by mink hounds. With pollution under strict supervision and control the eco-system is recovering. Otters have been seen on various sections of the river and bird life is being maintained. Although we can enjoy walking by certain sections of the river it is essential that some areas remain private and undisturbed so that the birds and animals can live and breed without intimidation.

A debt of gratitude is owed to men like Jim Coombes whose knowledge and advice will help to enhance and preserve the river for generations to come.

❧ Mills in Loddiswell Parish ❧

LODDISWELL MILL

Loddiswell Mill, like the other two mills in the parish, ground and graded flour from wheat for bread making, and barley for stockfeed, while oats were often rolled for horses and oatmeal for human consumption. The four pairs of stones were driven by two water wheels supplied with water channelled along a leat near Silveridge Wood from the River Avon.

The mill was owned by Thomas King around 1839, and by Francis Baker in the late 1870s. An advertisement in the *Kingsbridge Gazette* in 1892 states that it had recently been occupied by James Thomas:

Loddiswell Mill. To let yearly from Christmas day 1892 all those desirable Water, Grist and Flour Mills. Convenient dwelling house, Mill House, Malt House, Outhouses and Courtlage and about 17 acres of excellent Orchard and Pasture land now in the occupation of Mr James Thomas. Mills and Machinery very complete, working 4 pairs of stones driven by 2 water wheels, abundantly supplied with water from the River Avon. Capable of making 150 sacks of flour per week, Room for storing a quantity of corn & meal.
Malthouse capable of wetting 80 bushels of Malt.
Land of first quality.
Property close to proposed Railway Station on Kingsbridge line. About half a mile from Loddiswell and two and a half from Kingsbridge.

Viewing apply to Mr. John Prowse of Loddiswell. Sealed Tenders to the office of Messrs Square & Son, Kingsbridge before Friday 9th. Sept. 1892

The lease was taken by the Avon Milling Co., and from the turn of the century to the 1950s Holman and Son acquired the business and traded under that name. Local cereal crops were used for the production of flour, sharps and bran and for barley meal. Manures came into the area mainly by ship to be unloaded on the quayside at Kingsbridge, basic slag came from the iron foundries in the Midlands, Kainit from the potash mines in Europe and super phosphate in 2-cwt bags or in bulk from South America.

Francis Montgomery bought the redundant mill in 1959 and installed a Pelton-wheeled turbine and generator to produce heat and light for his newly-erected greenhouses, where market-garden crops were grown. The old Malt House between the cottages was disused for many years and has been converted into a granny flat.

In 1965 Julian and Mary Tregelles bought the premises and developed a garden centre there. The leat had deteriorated and became costly to maintain so the water turbine was removed and the mill building converted into four workshops; two on each floor and a flat for residential use.

The couple retired in 1997 and sold the business to Cheryl Chadwick who now runs the thriving garden centre with Andrew Flitcroft.

Loddiswell Mill, c.1936.

NEW MILL

It is not clear why it is so named, but New Mill had certainly been in operation for several centuries before the New Mill Bridge was built in 1893. The 1841 census records that the miller was Richard Willing who lived there with his wife, Amy, and their five sons and five daughters. One of the sons, William, married a girl named Avis and took over the mill in the 1850s. They had two daughters and then in June 1860 Avis died giving birth to a son who did not survive. William married again and in 1862 William Junr was born, the first of seven children (and Reg Sampson's grandfather). Three of the children were born at New Mill and in 1867 the family moved to North Mill, Slapton, where the next children were born.

The mill was advertised for sale in the *Kingsbridge Gazette* on 10 July 1869:

Sale Notice. Flour and Grist Mills. Machinery working three pairs of stones driven by a water wheel, supplying 100 sacks per week.
Dwelling house, Stabling, Piggeries, Courtlage, Garden, Orchard, Coppice and Waste.
Three closes making about 2 acres. Also the stone quarry with stone suitable for hardening

Right: Cliff Bye making a presentation to Mary Wesley at the Loddiswell Church Fête at New Mill, 1995.

Below: New Mill, 1930.

White's and *Kelly's Directories* stated that the miller in 1878 was James Adams and by 1897 Henry Hambley had taken over the business. His son, Edward, continued until he died and his widow, Louisa Hambley, kept the mill working from 1910 to 1939 with the help of mill worker Bill Barnes. Trade had decreased during this time and the business was discontinued from the beginning of the Second World War.

On the death of Mrs Louisa Hambley in 1948 the property was sold to Mrs Hope-Hudson who lived there with Monsieur Joubour. They began to improve the old buildings but sold it to Cecil Kitsell in 1955 who convened the mill and improved the domestic accommodation. Clifford and Priscilla Bye bought the property in 1984 and since then many church fêtes have been held there in the beautiful riverside gardens and lawns. The plastic duck race down the river has been one of the highlights of these events.

It is interesting to note that in 1850 the milling capacity at New Mill was equal to the output of the Town Mills at Kingsbridge and that the capacity of Loddiswell Mill was considerably larger again.

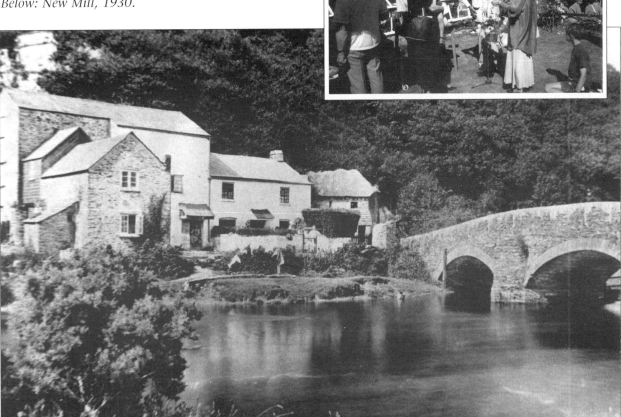

KNAP MILL

Wherever water could be made to drive a mill, it became a vital centre for the locality, turned at once to his own profit by the Lord of the Manor. For centuries Knap Mill was driven by water from Weeke which was diverted into a leat managed by a sluice at each end, then released back into the stream, discharging into the Avon just above the old fish-trap. The lane leading to it and named 'Miller's Path' is ancient, and must have seen an immemorial traffic of horses, plodding with a sack of corn slung over their backs and home again with the ground meal.

Equally important was the stamping machinery for fulling the homespun lengths of woollen cloth, woven on the handloom of nearly every cottage, in most cases, almost the only source of extra income. That Knap Mill served this dual role is certain, for the corn-grinding millstones are still there, and the large adjacent field, where the treated lengths were hung and stretched between tenterhooks, is called 'Rack Park'. Teasels are also still found in abundance.

The miller in 1839 was Alex Saunders and in November 1869 the property was advertised in the *Kingsbridge Gazette*:

Knap Mills, Loddiswell To let for 7 years, Flour and Grist Mills, Wheat and Barley mills, working 2 pairs of stones and 3 acres. To let by sealed tender.

It was leased to John Luscombe, miller, farmer and baker in Aveton Gifford. By 1897 his son, Servington Ward Luscombe, was continuing the business from the bakery in Aveton Gifford. James Moore was the miller by 1905 and lived at Knap Mill. His daughter, Edith, married John ('Jack') Elliott who was later badly injured in the First World War. The milling was continued by James Moore who farmed Knapp Mill and Cagford (near Yabbacombe) until 1935 as well as running the water mill. His grandson, Laskey Elliott, having mastered his trade at J.W.C. Scoble and Son, seized the opportunity in 1960 to employ his skills in his own business at the old mill by installing power-driven machines for the production of joinery in every form for local builders.

Top: James Moore and his wife and daughter Edith at Knap Mill, c.1912.
Above: James Moore's grandson, Laskey Elliott, began his joinery business at Knap Mill in 1959.

Malt Houses

White ale was produced in the brewhouse at the New Bridge Inn until the 1930s and in the second half of the 19th century there were two malt houses in Loddiswell Parish processing barley for ale production.

Vine Terrace in Town's Lane was a malt house owned by Richard and Amy Willing (née King). They lived in Vine House which, in 1831, had its thatched roof replaced with slates. The Malt Manager lived in Vine Cottage and the space between the two houses was where carts and wagons unloaded their barley.

In 1839 Richard Crocker built April Cottage in this space. He owned 'The Cottage' opposite and had bought Greystones Farm. When Richard Willing died in 1844 he left Vine House, Vine Terrace and some other properties to his son, William Willing Senr (born 1795). He died in 1852 leaving Little Reads to his wife Mary (née Luscombe) and Vine House, malt house, cottage, orchard and field to his son, William Willing Junr (born 1828). (These Willings were cousins of the family at New Mill.).

In 1856, William Willing Junr decided to sail to New Zealand so sold all his property including Treeby's and Higher, Lower and Three-cornered Pointridge' to his mother at Little Reads and set sail the following year. Deciding to join her son in 1861, Mrs Willing sold up to her nephew, Matthew (born 1841). Matthew Willing was declared bankrupt the following year, and his furniture was sold. His older brother, John Willing of Whitley, Thurlestone, bought the property and continued to make the malt.

The National Tax on malt in the 1860s aroused much resentment. John did not pay and was fined £200 for making malt without an Excise Licence. The Tax was swept aside in 1880 but this was too late for John who sold his properties in 1869, including Little Reads, to George Denbow and emigrated with his wife, Sarah, and brother, Richard, aboard the schooner *Yatala*.

John's debt had reputedly increased to £800 and in order to avoid the consequences it was decided to travel to the USA where their sister and her husband had lived since 1851. The journey must have been ill planned for after a short while at sea they discovered that the *Yatala* was carrying them to Australia. This was confirmed by John's great-grandson, Richard Willing, in 1997 when he and his wife, Celia, visited the UK.

When George Denbow died in 1872 the Town's Lane properties were bought by John Horton of East Allington, father of Trowbridge William Horton (Mrs Nellie Baker's father). 'Trow' as he was known, was a farmer and collected the rates from all property owners in the parish.

The other malt house in the parish was situated at Loddiswell Mill. It was 'capable of wetting 80 bushels of malt', and together these two malt houses could supply many of the white ale brewers in the district.

Vine Terrace converted from the old Malt House with Vine House on the left.

Rake Quarry, 29 March 1930. Back row (left to right): Edgar Edgecombe, Jack Eastley (Squire), Wilf Drew, Fred Luscombe (behind), Wilf Burman;
front: Jack Hawke, Mr Hawke, Mr and Mrs W.G. Northcott, Mr Jerred (Quarry Manager), Charlie Tarr, Cyril John Jefferies, Bill Luscombe, Ernest Hine, Bill Hine, Ern Luscombe, Bill Elliott, Bill Seldon.

Above left: Steam-roller on the Kingsbridge to Loddiswell road, 1950.

Above right: Presentation to Bill Taylor and Ern Luscombe by Bob Northcott, 1956.

Above: South Hams Quarry and Concrete Works, New Mill, Loddiswell, 1940.

Left: Bill Hine loading stone with a Ruston Bucyrus watched by Percy Johns, Quarry Foreman, 1954.

Chapter 16: Rake and Torr Quarries

William George Northcott resigned from Fothergill Bros. Contractors, Exeter, on 31 December 1928 and was restricted from being able to carry on contracting for a period of three years. He had been thinking about opening a quarry in South Devon for at that time, roadstone came to the district either by rail or sea. The rail-borne stone came from Teign Valley or from Tavistock; sea-borne stone from Cornwall. It was unloaded at Kingsbridge at the head of the creek and most of the boats were small barges or ketches with shallow draught. Mr Northcott had been purchasing stone from Cornwall for several years which he could sell to councils, some for tar-spraying to seal waterbound roads, so he had both funds and trade knowledge in his favour.

In 1928 he set about opening Rake Lower Quarry (Russell Baker's Yard). Negotiations were conducted with Richard Perraton of Rake Farm to obtain a lease to the quarrying rights on the farm. A plant was installed and began operating in 1929. Bill Hine began work there and the following year Charlie Tarr joined him leaving his farm work at Sorley. Bill Seldon Senr, a blacksmith at Newton St Cyres, and Arthur Grant, who supervised pile-driving for Fothergills, were recruited. Others soon joined the company, including Frank Quick, Harry Soper, Jim Hine and Wilfred Taylor.

It quickly became apparent that the good stone was covered by a thick layer of poor brown shale 'which would be costly to remove by physical labour'. Further up above the railway line it was known that a good mass of rock existed where the topping was much thinner. The best solution would be to haul the stone down by cart under the railway arch but Mr Perraton, the landowner, objected. The only way would be to construct an aerial gantry so that carrier buckets, clipped to the overhead cable, could cross over the railway and carry the stone from the new Rake Quarry to the crusher in the Lower Quarry. After quite a struggle, the railway company granted permission. The gantry began operation in March 1930.

The buckets carried about 4cwt of stone and were tipped into the crusher shute. The motive power for the crushing and screening plant was a 10 hp (nominal), portable steam engine run by Bill Elliott who had experience of travelling threshing plants which used steam tractors.

Stone chippings were sold for 13s.4d. a ton but within a few years the price dropped to 7s.10d. and did not recover until the Second World War. A quantity of quarry fines regularly accumulated near the crusher and was unsaleable so it was decided to use it to make concrete blocks. A site was found near Loddiswell New Bridge on the New Mill land and was quickly developed with Jim Hine as foreman. Wilfred Paynter was contracted to haul the dust to New Mill with his horse and cart. The first products were not up to the standard required but they were soon improved.

In the winter of 1936 trade was very difficult but the quarry was determined not to stand off the employees so other work was sought. William Roseveare of Plymouth, an architect, had been doing roadworks for developments in the Plymouth area. He had been engaged by Mr Archibald Nettlefold, a wealthy industrialist who had acquired Burgh Island and wished to extend the hotel there (which had been built in 1929). Northcotts obtained the contract to excavate the site and this excavated material had to be hauled up the island to the highest point and then tipped into a cove on the south side. The employees at Rake Quarry agreed to lodge on the island, returning home at the weekends. Charlie Tarr took charge of the works, arranged for housing and employed a cook. When work was completed the men returned to Rake.

Large quantities of stone were dug out from Rake Quarry and the possibilities of another site were considered. The first problem was to find enough stone to meet local authority requirements, since the new age of machine-broken stone was to replace numerous, locally hand-worked quarries for which the councils were directly responsible. In those days tenders were accepted for ripping stone from the quarries, hauling to roadside depots, hand breaking and eventually hauling to the steam-roller gangs.

Torr was to supply not only the broken stone but also various grades of tarmacadam. Construction of two sets of reinforced concrete bins, the installation of various primary and secondary crushers, screens and elevators, together with a tarmacadam plant was eventually complete and everything was set in motion during March 1936. A year later, in 1937, Rake Quarry was closed and the crusher and aerial gantry was dismantled and taken to Venn Quarry near Barnstaple.

Quarrying at Torr first commenced in a line with the old county workings where the stone was broken to a suitable size by 14lb sledge hammers, and thence loaded into Jubilee wagons for hauling, firstly driven by steam winch to the lower

Presentation to Charlie Tarr and Bill Seldon Senr by William Northcott at Torr Quarry, 1954. Left to right: Dennis Sharland, ? Crispin William (Bill) Hine, Tom Luscombe, Dennis Edgcombe, Tony Luscombe, Cyril Brooking, William (Bill) Stone, Leslie Auger, Sid Hine, George Williams, Raymond Laurey, Fred Hine, Glyn Brooking, Victor Hallett, Rupert Doyle, William Northcott, Jim Hine, Percy Johns, Charles Tarr, Ben Freeman, Cyril Jeffery Junr, Harry Withers, William (Bill) Seldon, Fred Riggall, Cyril Jeffery, Vic Drew, Fred Luscombe, Bill Edgecombe, Arthur Grant, Gerald Yeoman, Alfred Luscombe, Ernest Luscombe, Richard Perring, Jack Freeman, Leslie Hine.

Many Loddiswell men worked at the Devon County Quarry, Torr, in the late 1920s, including: George Soper (2nd left, back), Coulton Freeman (3rd left, front), Bill Hine (5th left, front), Frank Quick (7th left, front), Jim Hine (9th left, front), Wilf Taylor (10th left, front), Sid Hine (11th left, front).

level, and then by a further hoist up a one-in-four incline to the crushing and screening plant. These workings were subsequently found to be inadequate to meet increasing requirements and it was decided to work in the opposite direction to the old excavations and blast eastwards towards Torr Rock. This was successful and ample supplies of Blue Elvan stone have since been quarried.

Hammer and gad drilling at the old Rake was superseded at Torr by compressed-air-drilling machines, and steels which were forged, chiselled and tempered at the quarry blacksmith's shop by Bill Seldon Senr until hard enough to penetrate and stand up to the Elvan rock (the equivalent to granite). The quarry was gradually updated with a drill-sharpening machine and stone was blasted, plastered, loaded by excavator and conveyed by new dumpers to the main jaw crusher. The stone was then passed on for further crushing and screening to produce all the necessary grades and sizes. A 'Campbell' engine and later a 40hp. Vickers-Petter engine was installed until electrical power was introduced in 1942. At the same time the first Rapier 410 excavator was put into operation to remove quarry headings and deads, and assist in loading stone from the quarry face.

All of the men employed at Torr Quarry were drawn from the surrounding villages, many completing over 20 years' service when they received a gold watch. William (Bill) Hine received his in 1955 and on retiring in 1968 received a wrist watch from his colleagues. A dozen Hine family members have worked in the industry. Three generations of Jim Hine's family have taken pride in working in the quarry, and other Hines have chalked up two generations.

The company was registered as ECC Quarries

Ltd. on 19 December 1957. During the war another ECC Quarry at Berry Head received a request for stone from the War Department, later discovered to be in preparation for loading bays for D Day embarkation.

Glyn Brooking began work in the office at New Mill Concrete Works in 1938. He moved to Torr and then to the construction of the Royal Marine Centre at Lympstone. From 1940-46 he served in the RAF and then returned to Northcotts at Exeter. On 5 April 1947 Beryl Bowden and Glyn were married. He gained experience as Quarry Manager at Landrake and Greystone, and later at F. J. Moore Quarries. After open-heart surgery he retired to Shaldon, and died in 1991 after which Beryl returned to Loddiswell. Mr Bob Northcott recalls:

Recruits from the area proved to be most able, honest and loyal. They were a great bonus to our companies and no employer could ask for more... Arthur Grant was a brilliant man who could turn his hand to so many trades with great skill. He proved to be a guide and tutor to the young men who joined the firm. Glyn Brooking was another very able operator who became Director of the Company, a delightful person who... trained others in the industry. Horace Bailey, Fernleigh Pengelly, Ned Hine and George Williams all became successful and well-respected managers, and some directors. There were others too who became most able quarry foremen, who today would be called managers.

Torr Quarry closed in 1963 and some of the staff transferred to other Company quarries before retiring. Thus ended an important era in the industrial life of the village.

William and Selina Elliott started the bakery and grocery business in 1888.

Jack Hine, baker for Elliotts from 1947-76.

Grading and packing eggs at the South Hams Packing Station. Left to right: Anna Tolley, Emma Freeman, Hilda Brooking, Sheelagh Taylor, Joy Masters, Marjorie Jackson, Iris Wallbutton.

Chapter 17: Trades in Loddiswell

Bakers. Until about 1870 Loddiswell housewives did their own baking at home but by 1878 two ladies were baking bread for sale. Ten years later, in 1888, William Elliott began baking at a shop and premises in Fore Street. The London House Stores opposite was originally a pound for producing cider and was converted into a shop and bakehouse for Mr Barratt around 1900.

Elliotts

1878	Mrs Alice Bowden and Mrs Mary Denbow
1888	William Elliott, later William Henry Elliott
1930	John Richard Davis 1938 Rex Gerry
1947	Bert and Owen Elliott 1976 Peter Nathan
1982	Geoff Lewis (and Geoff Collins)
1987	John and Mary Pettit

London House Stores

1901	Mr Barrett 1906 John Yalland
1929	Reginald Ward; Powleslands
1959	Joseph L. Davies; Vascalini and Prior; Ken and Sylvia Pridham; Michael and Mary Piggott.

John and Mary Pettitt, bakers and grocers at the village shop since 1987.

Blacksmiths. John Kennard began as a blacksmith at Storridge and by 1850 worked at Virginia Cottage near the village pound. A disastrous fire broke out there in 1864 and raged through the five thatched cottages below. When the smithy was rebuilt the Kennards continued there until 1911 when they moved to Woodleigh and later to Kingsbridge. Fred Kernick, who trained at Widecombe, took on the business in 1911, later moving to a new smithy near Pointridge.

1839	Thomas Saunders (Village Centre)
1839	John Kennard (Storridge)
1839	Richard Jarvis (Little Gate)
1850	John Kennard, John Rundle W.P. Weeks
1878	John Kennard
1906	Frederick Kennard and Son
1911-61	Fred Kernick R.S.S.

Fred Kernick shown right with Johnny Brown and young Keith Hill from Ipplepen, 1936.

Butchers. Before abattoirs were regulated most villages had one or two butchers who served the community.

1839	Thomas Willing (Little Reads)
1850	Thomas Willing, James Yalland
1878	John Rossiter (and farmer) James Yalland (and farmer)
1897	Thomas Wakeham (Wyselands)
1906	Archibald Pitcher (Wyselands)
1927	Herbert George Walke (No.3 The Bank)
1966-77	Hobbs Brothers (No. 3. The Bank)

Thomas Wakeham by his butcher's shop at Wyselands, 1898.

CARPENTERS

1850	James Hine, John Hine, Jno. Popplestone, Philip Popplestone Robert Popplestone, John Prowse John Saunders (and painter)
1878	James Hyne, John Hyne, William Johns Robert Popplestone (and Parish Clerk) John Prowse (and wheelwright)
1897	John Hine, Phillip Popplestone
1906	Phillip Popplestone, John Prowse
1925	Henry (Harry) Rundle (and Undertaker, Hillside)
1955	Arthur Rundle (Hillside)

CARRIERS - HAULIERS

1878	John Guest, John Hyne (Timber Drawers) William Tallman (and farmer) Eli Yalland (and farmer)
1897	Charles Thomas (and farmer) Richard West, William H. Yalland Junr
1906	Richard West, Alfred Moore
1921	Arthur Preston, J.W. Hyne
& 1939	Walter John Guest (farm produce dealer)

DAIRYMEN

1906	Jas. Yalland Junr (Pointridge)
1939	James Yalland (Pointridge) Alfred Hingston (Ham Farm)
1957	Horace Griffin (Reads Farm) Richard (Dick) Lethbridge (Storridge)
1960	Cyril Harding (Wyselands)

MASONS

1850	William Bowden, Henry Stear, John Taylor
1878	John Pedrick, John Pedrick Junr, John Prowse
1890-1935	Bob Yabsley
1925-35	Tom Squires

GAME DEALER

| 1897 | Richard Knight |

LAUNDRESSES

| 1897 | Miss Elizabeth Popplestone, Mrs Mary Saunders |
| 1906 | Miss Elizabeth Popplestone |

MALSTERS

1839	Richard Willing (Vine Terrace)
1850	William Willing (and farmer, Little Reads)
1862	John Willing (Vine Terrace)

MILLERS

1850	Thomas King (Loddiswell) Alex Saunders (Knap) Richard Willing (New Mill)
1878	James Adams (New Mill) Francis Baker (Loddiswell Mill) John Luscombe (Knap Mill)
1897	Avon Milling Co. (Loddiswell Mill), Henry Hambly (New Mill) Servington Ward Luscombe (Knap Mill)
1906	Edward Hambly (New Mill), Holman & Sons (Loddiswell Mill)
1939	Mrs Louisa Hambly (New Mill), Holman & Sons (Avon Mill)

POST OFFICE

1843-93	James Harvey then Jasper Harvey (Prospect Cottage)
1897	George Yalland (Fore Street – part of Elliott's) Susie Kennard
1915	William Bush married Dorothy Clayton (Postmistress with niece Molly, Fore Sweet)
1947-55	Glyn and Beryl Brooking (Whitelocks)
1955	Arthur and Florence Burdett (Whitelocks)
1960	Wilfred and Jessie Batten (Whitelocks)
1963	Reginald and Sarah Pike
1972	Peter and Carol Newman
1977	George Morton
1981-1997	Ronald and Pauline Tomlinson
1998	John and Sheila Hornsby

John and Jasper Harvey's shoe maker's shop and Post Office at Mount Pleasant (Prospect Cottage on right).

PUBLICANS

TURKS HEAD

1850	Thomas Rundle
1878	Thomas Rundle
1878	Aaron Luscombe (Church House Inn)
1897	William Henry Rundle
1906	Alfred Herbert Stigings
1910-31	Robert Yabsley
1931	Cyril Oldrieve
1935	William Thomas Rundle
1941-45	Bill Pavey
1945	Sam Griffin
1950	Frank and Ailsa Cherry
????	Edward George Gillow
1966	Kenneth John Jasper
1971	John and Joyce Kirby
1977	Robert and Gillian Pearce
1975	Trevor and Sandra Wilson
1976	Vacant

Turks Head renamed Loddiswell Inn

1978	Arthur and Vera Whittle
1984	Graham and Linda Richardson
1985	Gerald and David Lamb
1987	Kathleen Jinks
1988	Ziggi Addey
1990	John and Hazel White
1996	Ronald and Kathleen Shopland
1998	Roger and Sally Pinder

Gladys Eastley outside the New Bridge Inn, c.1940.

New Bridge Inn

1839	Thomas Rundle
1850	John Tallman
1878	Mrs M.Tallman
1897-1917	Mrs Tryphena Lakeman
1917-43	Walter John Guest
1943-46	Iris Wallbutton and Sheelagh Taylor
1946	Walter Hingston
	Bert and Doreen Christopher
1960	William and Catherine Brewer
1962	Albert and Myra Hopper
1964-81	William and Alice Loram
1982	Michael Olney
1986	Arthur Whittle (Manager)
1988	New Bridge Inn closed

Top: Turks Head with John Yalland's baker's shop in the background, 1920.
Above: Bob and Selina Yabsley, proprietors of the Turks Head Inn 1910-31.

ROAD CONTRACTOR

1878   James Wills Prowse (and farmer)

SEXTONS

1878	Richard Lane.
1892-1947	William Hingston.
1947	John Brown

SHOE AND BOOT MAKERS

1850	John Harvey
	John Hoskin
	Thomas Yalland (Prospect Cottage)
1878	Jasper Harvey (farmer/Postmaster)
	John Preston
	William Yalland
1897	John Preston
	William Henry Yalland (Fir Cottage)
1906	John Preston
	William Preston
	Mrs Mary Ann Yalland (Fir Cottage)
1924-63	Herbert Bowden (No. 1 The Bank)

Bert Bowden at work in his shop, 1950.

SHOPKEEPERS

1850	John Guest
	Henry Lake
	John Lidstone
1878	William Frigall (and farmer)
	Amelia Lidstone (grocer and draper),
	Alexander Luscombe (grocer, draper, tailor, farmer)
1897	James Lapthorne (draper, grocer)
	William Harvey Sloggett (grocer, draper)
1906	James Lapthorne (draper, grocer)
1910-47	Miss Rosa Preston
1935	Ida Hawke (Silveridge)
1944-88	Sydney and Winnie Jeffery
1996	Michael and Reeta Price

Ward's Shop and Fore Street, 1930.

TAILORS

1850	Henry B. Lake
	Richard Lidstone
	William Lidstone
	George Luscombe
1878	William Lidstone
1897	Peter Rogers
	James Yalland
1906	Peter Rogers

THATCHERS

1850	John Gay
1878	Richard Rogers
	Thomas Rundle (and Turk's Head)
1935	Charlie Watts

THRESHING AND AGRICULTURAL CONTRACTORS

1927-47	Alan and Henley Baker (Hazelwood) Jack Baker (Warcombe)

WATER BAILIFF

1897	Alfred Martin
	Charlie Stabb
	Sgt Hawkins

WHEELWRIGHTS

1850	Elias Sandover
1878	Elias Sandover
	John Prowse (and carpenter)
1897	John Winsor Sandover
	Edwin Wood
1906	John Winsor Sandover

John Winsor Sandover inspecting his bees in 1921.

WOOLCOMBER
(Prepared fleeces for spinning worsted, necessary for cloth making)

1850 John Hill

YELLOW OCHRE MANUFACTURERS
(Blended red and yellow ochre for cottage decoration)

1850 Jno and Henry Luscombe
(Blackdown Farm)

Craftsmen, Building Contractors and Commerce. During the first half of the 20th century most houses had outside sanitation and water was fetched from a communal pump or standpipe. A few new houses were built in the village, such as Silveridge, Pointridge and Chevithorne, but most others were just maintained or slightly improved.

The spate of house-building after the Second World War generated the need for building contractors who, in turn, required the newer skills of plumbers and electricians. The introduction of the New Planning Controls in 1950 created work for specialised architects and quantity surveyors.

Prefabricated bricks and blocks were used instead of stone, and the materials for block making and road improvements expanded the quarrying industry. Loddiswell people have provided most of these skills in the second half of the 20th century:

Bert and Jane Taylor, John Webber & Sons
　(Robert and Kevin), Basil Taylor and
　Rodney Brooking, Michael Hine (contractors)
Laskey Elliott, Roderick Elliott (carpenters)
Vic Ibbetson, Shaun Taylor (carpet fitters)
Hatch Craft Centre, Mark Arnold (craft centres)
Steve Yabsley (computer specialist)
John Marsh, Brian Pope, Graham Hodge,
　Anthony Treeby, Kerry Taylor (electrical
　contractors)
Russell Baker (engineer)
Avon Mill Nurseries, M.G.M. Nurseries
Peter Jeffery (holiday home maintenance)
Hatch Marquees (Richard and Anita Ling)
Bill Rockey, Andrew Tickner, Andrew
Edgcombe, Mark Taylor (painters and
　decorators)
Gordon Rundle, Brian Rundle, Andy Hurrell
　(plumbers)
Steve Dutton (photography)
Derek Brooking (plant hire)

At the turn of the century, Loddiswell still harbours many of the traditional old trades and professions. There are carpenters, gardeners, farmers, publicans and schoolteachers, and to these have been added the skills born of the 20th century. The village has computer experts, graphic designers, photographers, electricians, television presenters and many other enterprises which allow those who spurn city life to make a living in Loddiswell's beautiful rural surroundings.

Sometimes events seem to turn full circle. The 1878 directory records that two wheelwrights were at work in the village. Many of the older inhabitants remember John Sandover and his workshop (now converted to a dwelling house) in the main street where he was kept busy repairing cart wheels, which were vital to the transport system. Incredible as it may seem, one of only 50 wheelwrights practising in the British Isles today has his workshop in the parish. Mark Arnold, the present owner of the Great Barn at Hatch, has converted the building into a centre for rural crafts. He is still occasionally required to make a wheel for a cart, but most of his work is involved in specialist carpentry and cabinet-making. There is also at work in Hatch a shoemaker, a potter, a photographer and a furniture restorer.

Loddiswell has always been a base for commercial activities, some fulfilling the needs of the community, others geared towards more diverse production and distribution. Richard West was a carrier who drove his horses and wagon between Loddiswell and Kingsbridge hauling anything from groceries to medicine. Some years later Arthur Preston transported people to the market town of Kingsbridge in his Morris van, equipped with movable benches on either side. Up to a dozen adults and children would squeeze in for the 10am journey and were happy to make the return at 4pm. Sometimes the seats were pulled out to make an extra journey to market with a few calves. The Western National Omnibus Company improved its services when the railway closed in 1963 but many journeys are now taken by car or taxi.

Sydney and Winnie Jeffery moved into a flat at Sunnyside in 1944 and converted the stables underneath into a shop for the sale of hardware and it was here that Sydney continued his clock-repairing business. By 1952 it was apparent that the village needed a petrol station to service the increasing number of cars so tanks and pumps were installed. Winnie recalls that their first customer was Norman Rogers of Ham Farm for the pool petrol which was rationed by coupons and cost 1s.11d. per gallon. The business continued with the help of their son, Peter, from 1952 to 1988 when the station was closed and the site sold for residential development.

Many Loddiswellians were employed at the quarries and at the egg packing station but both have long since closed. The haulage firms of W. J. Guest and J.W. Hyne have been superseded and the commercial employment base has moved from the village to Robin's Park Industrial Centre near Loddiswell Butts. It was developed by Brooking Properties and others, and provides stores and workshops for Derek Brooking and his earth-moving and plant hire business. Nigel Hall runs a Haulage enterprise and next door Peter Sweet of P & R Motors has a car repair garage. Malborough Packaging, owned by Jim and Susan Carr, employ about 25 people making and supplying induction foils and standard bottle cap liners (*below*). In 1998 work began on another workshop for Frank Broadheard and Son for their plant hire firm.

CIDER

Cider presses of Loddiswell Parish have included: Yanston Farm, Coombe Farm, Great Gate Farm, Hatch Farm, Reeds Farm, Wigford Farm, Tunley Farm, Old Vicarage and the site of the London House Stores.

George Shepherd of Yanston was one of the chief cider makers in the South Hams until the late 1940s. The crusher was originally driven by a horse and later by an oil engine. The full-size timber press was filled with apple pulp between layers of reed or hessian before the square platform was pressed down by two men pushing a ratcheted lever to and fro. As the pressure increased, the apple juice ran into a stone trough and was then transferred into hogsheads (54 gallon casks) for fermentation.

Willow plots in the parish in 1839 included: Hatch, Weeke, Yanston, Alleron, Stanton and Reveton. The willows were grown for basket making – stripped of their bark for the white, square market baskets or unstripped for black baskets or maunds for carrying mangolds to feed the housed cattle during the winter. Some willows were sold for making crab pots.

SOUTH HAMS PACKING STATION

(WRITTEN IN 1970

BY JULYAN TAYLOR, AGED NINE)

This business was started by my great-grandfather W. J. Guest in 1921. He was born September 1st 1886 and lived at 1 Ethel Cottages, The Bank, Loddiswell. He attended Loddiswell British School (Congregational). He worked with his brother on the stage coach that ran between Kingsbridge and Dartmouth via Torcross. He married Joan Mary Mcleod, a nurse at the London Hospital, White Chapel Road. She was in the background urging him on and was his inspiration. He had the idea of visiting the farms and persuading farmers to sell him all of their milk which he sold to Torquay Co-operative Society. The milk business began in 1921 and W. J. Guest was the first person to buy bulk milk in the South West of England.

W. J. Guest also collected and sold dairy produce. He started the egg packing business based at the Courtledge. The egg packing station has up-to-date machinery. First the eggs are collected and tested, they are packed and put into cardboard boxes and labelled Large, Standard, Medium or Small. Each box holds 30 dozen eggs. They can deal with 250 boxes a day. The poultry department can deal with more than 1000 birds a day, which are sent to hotels, butchers, shops and stores over a wide area. Eggs and poultry are collected in a radius of 30 miles of the packing station. The eggs are sent to London, Brighton, Hove, St Leonard's, Hastings, the Isle of Wight, Poole and Bournemouth.

W. J. Guest died in 1942 and my Grandmother, Mrs S.R. Taylor, and my Aunt, Mrs I.K. Wallbutton, are now carrying on the business with other members of the family. Each member of the family has a special responsibility in running the business. One member of the family at Belle Vue Farm, Kingston, supplies chicken for the poultry section. She and her husband, Mr David Freeman, rear 10 000 chickens in two houses.

There are over 30 staff employed by the egg packing station and they come from Kingston, Kingsbridge and Loddiswell. The egg packing station is an architect-designed building and it has local stone frontage to match its surroundings.

Staff at the plant, left to right: Audrey Pope, Gillian Robinson, Marion Eastley, Lina Marsh, Joyce Lethbridge, Anna Tolley, Sandra Hine, Hilda Brooking, Geoffery Lilley.

141

J.W. HYNE LTD, HAULAGE CONTRACTOR
(BY RICHARD HYNE AGED TEN, 1969)

My Grandfather, J.W. Hyne, started the business using a horse and cart in the year 1919. The first lorry that the business had was in 1929. The business was made a limited company in March 1965 and was known as J.W. Hyne Ltd. Six families work in the business. There were four different weights of lorries – one 20 ton, one 16 ton, one 10 ton and a 9 ton lorry. The four smaller lorries work at quarries, three at Torr Quarry and one at Launceston in Cornwall.

The other lorries go to London, the Midlands, Hull and Manchester. The things they carry are road materials, tarmac, Chipping's, etc. and house-building materials, including bricks, blocks and sand. All these materials come from the local quarries. English China Clay is hauled from Cornwall to London by a lorry which often brings back fertilisers from Buckingham and coal from the Midlands (this goes to Buckfastleigh Mills.) Cauliflowers, lettuces, cabbages and strawberries from France are taken to the Midlands and various commodities are brought back from Hull, such as baths, radiators, crates and oil drums.

One of Jack Hyne's pre-war lorries.

A.S. JEFFERY CLOCK MAKER AND WATCH REPAIRER (BY JOHN JEFFERY, 1969)

The church clock was made by a Mr Richard Wills of Truro between 1750 and 1790. In 1962 the clock stopped and Loddiswell people became quite concerned. They wanted to know if it would have to be replaced by a new clock and were concerned about the cost. Clock makers said it would have to be replaced and would cost about £400. My father, Mr A.S. Jeffery, said he would try to repair it at an estimated cost of about £60. He took the clock to bits and carried it down the tower steps. He had to make some parts for it and then took it up the steps again and assembled it in the tower. The clock is now in working order and has worked ever since.

THE HOME BAKERY
(BY GARRY ELLIOTT AGED 10, 1969)

The bakery was started in 1888 by my great-grandfather and has been in our family for about 85 years. The bread was made by hand until electricity was brought to Loddiswell. My grandfather and great-grandfather made about 90 to 100 4lb loaves and about 70 8lb loaves every day in about 1900. Now in 1969 we make about 50 1lb and about 200 2lb loaves. The old price of loaves was 4-4½d. for a 4lb loaf and 8-9d. for an 8lb loaf. We cover around a 4 mile radius with the vans.

The first method of travel was a 'kit'; it was like a wheelbarrow with three wheels and without sides except for the front to stop the groceries from falling out, and metal bars for the sides. Then my grandfather went to Torquay and bought a horse and trap, and after that we had motor vans.

The village people used to bring their dinners to be cooked in the oven on the square tiles. Coal was used for fuel for the three ovens in Loddiswell but now there is only one. There are eight people employed and they make 200 pasties a day on Wednesdays and Thursdays.

Chapter 18: Royal and National Celebrations

The people of Loddiswell have always celebrated royal occasions in a grand style, with a lavish supply of food and drink.

In 1863 on the marriage of Edward, Prince of Wales (later Edward VII) and Princess Alexandria of Denmark, Loddiswell put on a wonderful display of decorations with five triumphal arches across the main road and two leading to the church: one of these near the Terrace consisted of two towers united in an arch. In the middle was a shield 5 feet high bearing the royal arms, surrounded by flags and portraits of the royal couple.

Queen Victoria's Golden Jubilee in 1887 was celebrated in a similar way and the event recorded (on 21 June) by the Secretary of the Organising Committee:

On May 10th a meeting was held in the National Schoolroom to consider the ways and means of celebrating the Queen's Jubilee. F.W Weymouth Esq., was elected to the chair and subscriptions to the amount of £11.10 were then and there promised towards the feast... As time went on, subscriptions increased in magnitude to about £60, which was considered sufficient to give a free dinner and tea to all the inhabitants of the parish. Accordingly the undermentioned Committees were chosen, and one and all set to work to carry out the day's proceedings. The Committees consisted of:
Sports: Messrs A. Luscombe; J. Rossiter; Rev. F. Boultbee,W. Tallman; F.W. Weymouth Esq., N.T. Rogers; Col Wise; T. Willing; C. Thomas, J. Thomas; A. Parker; F. Wakeham, F. Kennard; W. Shepherd.
Decorations: J. Popplestone; Adams; J.Yalland; F. Coombe, Secretary; P. Foale, Treas.
The Band: Messrs J. Tapp, Bandmaster; J. Prouse; W. Elliott; W. Hingston; R. Yabsley; W. Preston; J. Popplestone; R. Popplestone; R. Skinner; J. Mortimer.

The early morn of Jubilee Day was ushered in by a merry peal on the Church bells. The weather was beautiful fine, as it had been for three weeks previous, but the roads were very dusty. The decorations were begun on the 20th. June and continued up to eleven o clock of the 21st.

Procession
At 11.30 am a Procession was formed at Ham Butts. A large Banner with a crown and the word "Jubilee 1887" on it was carried in front of the Brass Band which was followed by the two Schools side by side. The Union Jack was followed by the adult population numbering about four hundred carrying numerous flags, and marching to Church by way of Terrace Hill.

Church Service
The Church was filled to overflow. The service used was that appointed by the authorities, and conducted by the Rev. F.T. Boultbee. Mr. F. Coombe, dissenting minister, read the lesson. The Church and Chapel choirs sang together, and each part was supported by an instrument from the Brass Band, and the drum, together with the organ which was played by Mr. J. Tapp.

Dinner
After Service the Procession marched to the New Road, which is at present closed to the public, where dinner was laid on tables lent by the villagers. Grace was sung and accompanied by the Band. The dinner consisted of cold roast and boiled beef, roast pork and bread, followed by plum pudding.
The Committee, carvers and waiters dined after the others in the veranda of the British Schoolroom. Provision was made for 600 but not more than 500 attended the feast. A fat bullock was bought of Mr R. Rogers of Woolston, West Alvington, which weighed over 6 cwt. for £18, and bread was bought for four and a halfpence for a four pound loaf.

Sports
After dinner sports were carried on in a field kindly lent by Mr F. Willing of Tunley, comprising Hurdle races; Steeple chases; Wheelbarrow races; Obstacle and Three-legged races; and Flat races for women and girls. Long and high jumps, putting the weight, and donkey racing, scrambling for nuts and sweets, and dancing. Nearly £5 was given in prize money.

TEA

Tea was laid on the same tables as dinner. The provisions were 3 cwt. of cake, tough-cakes, tea and butter The following list of ladies superintended the Tea: Mesdames: Lidstone; (Hazelwood) Nichol; Wakeham; Maunder; Shepherd; Rogers; Lidstone; Prowse; Walke; Weymouth; Yalland; Adams; Willing (Reads) Thomas; Hodder; Widger; Harvey; Baker; Laskey; Boultbee. Misses Parnell; Helms; Parker; Wise.

DECORATIONS

Six arches spanned the streets at different parts. The principal one, and an elaborate piece of workmanship, and deserving special notice, was fixed at the higher end of the New Road and bore the motto "God Save the Queen" in large blue letters on while calico, surmounted with a massive crown artistically made; beneath the crown was suspended a fine portrait of Queen Victoria, and fir trees were planted on either side of the arch. Another at The Terrace bore an inscription "Victoria Regina"and Victoria crosses, with a very pretty anchor suspended from the crown of the arch. Flags were mounted on the tower and other... buildings: the whole gave the village a very gay and holiday like appearance. The decorations remained intact to the end of the week.

DRINK

Six 'kilderkins' of beer (18 gallon barrels) were provided, but five only were used.

BONFIRE AND FIREWORKS

A huge bonfire was lit at the Rings on Blackdown about 10pm. While the fire was burning rockets were let off by Col. Wise, and coloured lights by the Rev. F. T. Boultbee. The band played, and dancing was kept up by the light of the bonfire till 12 o' clock, when the band played the National Anthem. Thus ended the gayest holiday ever remembered in Loddiswell.

On the following day the fragments of meat and bread were sold and pudding given away; and cake distributed to the two Schools.

GOD SAVE VICTORIA

Above: Listening to the opening announcement of the Silver Jubilee Celebrations by the Reading Room, May 1935.

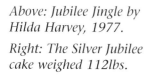

Above: Jubilee Jingle by Hilda Harvey, 1977.

Right: The Silver Jubilee cake weighed 112lbs.

Ten years later in 1897 Queen Victoria's Diamond Jubilee provided another opportunity to celebrate.

There were two special days in the 1930s to lift the spirits of the population after the Great Depression. King George V and Queen Mary reached the Silver Jubilee of their reign in 1935 and then, following the death of King George, came the Coronation of King George VI and Queen Elizabeth in 1937.

Since then parishioners have had Queen Elizabeth II's Coronation in 1952 and, more recently, the Silver Jubilee in 1977 to remember. The latter was celebrated in the Courtledge using the former egg packing station for the presentation of the Jubilee mugs to the babies and schoolchildren, and the cutting of the the Jubilee Cake. It was made by Betty Sampson and iced by Sheila Elliott, and weighed 112 lbs (50 kg), measuring 42 by 24 inches. The ingredients cost £43.20:

9 lbs Butter	10 lbs caster sugar
3 lbs mixed peel	4.5 lbs seeded raisins
12 lbs sultanas	12 lbs plain flour
1 teaspoon salt	3 teasp mixed spice
half pint brandy	60 eggs
15 lbs currants	4.5 lbs Glace cherries
4.5 lbs sweet chopped almonds	
quarter pint lemon juice	

Icing:

10 lbs icing sugar   14lbs almond paste

Houses and gardens throughout the village were decorated and judged in a competition by Christian Michell and Lavinia Parish. A chain of bonfires was lit, started by the Queen at Windsor Castle at 10pm and lit on the Blackdown Rings at 10.15pm.

Armada 400, celebrated in 1988, began with the ringing of the church bells with most of the events taking place at the Blackdown Rings. A large bonfire had been built on the highest point and was lit in succession with others along the English Channel coast. It provided light for a barbecue and the many stalls of food and drink. From Wembury to Torquay, around the coast, and into Dartmoor one could count 14 other beacons lighting the night sky.

The 50th Anniversary of VE Day was held in 1995 when the bells rang out before and after a Service of Thanksgiving at the church. During the morning a competition for decorated windows was judged by Alison Withnell and was won by Eunice Yabsley.

The Courtledge was a hive of activity in the afternoon where a variety of fancy dresses were judged (*above*). The schoolchildren performed several country dances led by Hilary Hudson on her accordion. David Jeffery on his accordion then struck up some old wartime songs and everyone lustily joined in. Later both musicians led the old time dancing.

Before the buffet tea, prepared by the village community and served by the Women's Institute, the schoolchildren, toddlers and babies were presented with a specially-minted £2 coin. Once again Betty Sampson made an enormous cake which was iced by Angela Freeman. The day was beautifully warm and sunny allowing adults and children to take their tea sitting on the grass.

Judges at the VE Day celebrations, 1995. Left to right: Cyril Brooking, Capt William Peek, Dennis Sharland.

VE Day Anniversary 1995

Above and right: Relaxed spectators at the VE Day celebrations in the Courtledge, 1995.

Above: Bill Kitts cutting the cake which measured 4ft by 2ft.

Right: Children dancing to Hilary Hudson's accordion.

Chapter 19: Entertainment and Leisure

CHRISTIAN MICHELL AND THE VILLAGE PLAYERS

Christian Michell came to Loddiswell as a primary school teacher in 1935 and her contribution to village life over the following 50 years was enormous. She was a teacher at the school until 1972 and will be remembered for the quality of her tuition and her great sense of humour.

Her interest in drama prompted her to write pantomimes for the village in the late 1930s and early '40s. Her wonderful *Cinderella* was a great success playing to full houses at Loddiswell before performing at the Town Hall, Kingsbridge.

These were the forerunners of a series of plays which followed in the post-war years. They were performed before audiences in Loddiswell, and on invitation at Kingsbridge and Ivybridge. Christian Michell was a great disciplinarian and every one had to be sure of their lines by the final rehearsal. Needless to say everyone joined in the celebrations after the show.

Peacemakers was based on the conflict in the minds of young people about pacifism at the time of the Munich Crisis. *Red Earth*, based on the South Devon Evacuation Area, received national recognition and has since been performed as far afield as Australia.

In later years her indefatigable energy was devoted to following her interest in local history and genealogy. She was helped in her research by Margaret Common, her life-long friend who had been headteacher at Loddiswell School from 1936 to 1970. Together they travelled to record offices at Exeter and sometimes London in order to establish the true facts. They could be relied upon to trace the history of nearly every family, not only in Loddiswell, but in the surrounding district.

Peacemakers, 1948. Left to right: Florence Todd, Betty Sampson, Dorothy Taylor (behind), Eva Kernick, Arthur Grant, Betty Lethbridge, Hilary Field, Owen Rundle, Gladys Hodge, John Mabin (behind), Beryl and Glynn Brooking, Hazel Mabin, Reg Sampson, Seymour Luscombe, Eddie Mabin (behind), Basil Taylor.

Right: Red Earth, 1946. Left to right: Betty Lethbridge, Eva Kernick, Betty Sampson, Dorothy Parsliffe, Florence Todd, Glyn Brooking, Hazel Grant, Reg Sampson, Gladys Hodge, Owen Rundle, John Mabin, Hilary Field.

Cinderella at Kingsbridge Town Hall, 1940.

Back row (left to right): Bert Elliott, Sylvia Tout, Susan Hannah, Violet Mabin, Arthur Preston, Christian Michell, Ethel Eastley, Phyllis Harding, Eva Kernick, Jack Eastley, Bert Bowden and Arthur Grant (horse), Florence Todd, Dorothy Taylor, Bill Taylor;

front row: Betty Lethbridge, Ivy Brooking, Rose Preston, Rene Marshall, Sheelagh Taylor, Marion Hyne, Mrs Thrasher, Mabel Gerry, Queenie Hingston, Gladys Hodge;

girls kneeling: Valerie Tout, Hazel Grant, Sylvia Hingston.

LODDISWELL HORTICULTURAL SHOW AND SPORTS SOCIETY

From the beginning of the 20th century householders were encouraged to be self-sufficient in garden produce as fresh fruit and vegetables helped to provide a healthy diet for the growing family.

The Loddiswell Cottage Garden Society was formed on 5 March 1909 so that lectures could be held on new and established practices in vegetable growing and to arrange competitive shows in the spring and summer in the Village Hall. The classes to be judged were: allotments and cottage gardens, fruit, flowers, vegetables, honey, poultry, butter, cream, eggs. Sports were held on the same day, 2

John Common encouraging the Junior Tug-of-War, 1964.

August, in a field of Court House on the east side of the top of Terrace Hill, for athletic sports, a comic race and a 2 mile pony race over a jump, six times around the field. Tea was provided on the sports field at 6d. per head.

The following year, 1910, the show and sports were expanded, a class for ducks was added to the poultry section and the Rev. Hodges gave prizes for children's flowers in water. On the field a brick wall, a gate and six flights of hurdles were used for horse jumping and an enclosure for 'Gentlemen' was constructed with a notice on the adjoining hayrick. No mention of 'Ladies'.

Mr Cutler, the Showman, was admitted with swing-boats, hoopla and a sweet stall for a fee of 10 shillings The corn merchant, M. Holman, lent 20 sacks for the sack race and Mr Ford organised 'putting the weight'. A few years later a competition to judge the weight of a pig began, and young people displayed maypole dancing. Mr Hodder of Great Gate offered his barn for a show dance.

The First World War caused disruption and no shows were held from 1915 to 1921 when the Society was renamed the Loddiswell Horticultural Society. Loddiswell gardeners became highly proficient in growing the longest parsnips and the largest marrows, and guarded the secrets of their success very carefully. Cottagers could be seen late at night with an oil lantern in one hand and a pail

of secret brew in the other, watering their precious crop until the appointed day. Success at Loddiswell Show encouraged many to compete elsewhere.

The horticulture and panniery was transferred from the Village Hall to a marquee in the sports field in 1931. The tender from H. J. Gray was £10.4s.6d. for a marquee 30 foot by 90 foot. Mr W.G. Northcott offered £10 prize money to bona fide quarrymen in the district and tug-of-war teams were arranged between Rake and Torr. These quarry classes and teams were discontinued in 1958 when the quarries closed. The class for the 'Best Pair of Farm Horses' was changed to the 'Best Single Farm Horse Confined to the Parish'. The Kingsbridge Silver Band was engaged as usual at a fee of £7.10s. and the Melody Makers Dance Orchestra provided music for the dance in the evening at £2.

By the late 1930s darts had become popular in the public houses of the district and in 1938 W.G. Northcott suggested that an inter-pub competition should be held on the field.

The Second World War caused a lapse in the staging of the Show and Sports of six years until 1946 and in 1947 they moved across from the Court House fields to the newly-acquired playing fields. Bert Elliott resigned in 1951 as Secretary after 23 years of service and became Director of the Show with Reg Sampson as Field Manager.

Coronation Year in 1953 was presided over by the second generation of quarry owners, W.R. Northcott and, in anticipation of the erection of the new pavilion and toilet block, only one Elsan was ordered from Topes 'for the Ladies'!

In 1969 a presentation was made to L.R. Sampson in recognition of 45 years of service, including 20 years as Chairman. The year 1967 had been a crisis year. Many of the older committee members had resigned or left the area, and it was decided that no Show should be held that year. This generated a surge of interest from younger members of the community and the structure of the Show and Sports was reviewed. Horse judging and jumping, which had dominated the field, was discontinued giving

Territorial Army Tug-of-War Team, Loddiswell Show, 1930 (left front is Jack Hodge).

The start of the Pony Race at Loddiswell Show, 30 July 1925.
Left to right: Bob Popplestone, Jim Hine, Harry Yabsley, Richard Perraton.

much-needed time and space for the more popular gymkhana. Side shows and a family dog show were introduced and each year a special feature formed the main attraction: a traction engine and thresher, wagons and traps, veteran and vintage cars or motor cycles. The crafts of spinning, weaving and dyeing, cane and rush basket making, lace, pottery and falconry were also displayed. Police dog demonstrations and archery, wrought-ironwork and horse shoeing, free-fall parachuting and radio-controlled model aircraft have all contributed to the success of the Show through the years.

There have always been many contenders for the Loddiswell Mile and since 1987 five-a-side football has proved to be very popular. Children have enjoyed the clowns or the Punch and Judy show, and are eager to try their hands at skittles or welly throwing.

The 50th anniversary of Loddiswell Show was celebrated in 1971 when members dressed in Edwardian costumes, over 100 hired from Torquay and Bristol. The President, Bert Elliott, came to the Show in a horse-drawn market trap and was followed by schoolchildren riding on a farm wagon. At the end of the day Bert Francis, a retired London photographer, recorded the event with his full plate camera. Our great-grandparents who initiated the first Loddiswell Show nearly a century ago would not recognise it in its present form. Vegetables still play an important part in the Show display, but flowers and flower arranging have transformed the marquee into a place of glorious splendour, with domestic science and homecraft replacing dairy and poultry products. The emphasis has moved towards entertainment for both young and old, but one aspect remains unchanged – it is the pleasure of meeting friends and neighbours on this Special Loddiswell Show Day. Long may it continue!

Above: Left to right: Len Wood, Jim Hine, Harold Lethbridge and Dennis Hine discussing the judges' decision in the vegetable competition, 1988.

Below: Children arriving at the Loddiswell show on a farm wagon for the 50th anniversary, 1971. Left to right: Yvonne Lethbridge, Anne Harvey, Maurice Sampson, Elaine Penman, Sally Clarke, Andrew Lethbridge, Trevor Reeve, Christine Brooking.

Above: Russell Baker, organiser for the motorcycle display.

Loddiswell Show

Loddiswell Show Produce and Field Committee and Stewards, 1964.
Back row (left to right): Dennis Cliff, Dennis Hine, Richard Storey, Michael Marshall, Bill Rose, Leslie Walke, ? (Produce Judge), Edith and Charles Storey, Bert Elliott (behind), Dr Rogers, Gareth Haylett, Sydney Scoble, Lewis Reg Sampson (front), Leonard Scobell (behind), Harry Yabsley, Peter Carpenter, Reg Sampson, Cyril Harding, Harold Eastley;
front: Terry Marshall, Arthur Preston, Dick Perring, Frank Carpenter, Roy Scobell, John Commons, Fred Parsliffe.

Far right:
Vegetable display, 1998.

Right and below: Hilda Harvey and Violet Hine with their prize-winning gardens, 1996.

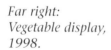

Right: The winners of the five-a-side football competition being presented with awards by John Nash (President), assisted by Mrs Patricia Bazzano (Chairperson), 1998.

The 50th anniversary of Loddiswell Show in 1971 celebrated in Edwardian costumes.
(Left to right) back: Arthur Brimacombe, Adrian Lethbridge, Ian Jenkinson, Tim Dickinson, John Sampson,
Frank Carpenter, John Hallmark, John Johnson, Dennis Hine, Dennis Cliff;
4th row: Bill Walters, Sara Field, Joan Parsons, Margaret Foulkes, May Joint, Gordon Beckley, Jamie Hyne,
Steward Hyne, Bill Hine, Rev. Herbert Jefferson;
3rd row: Pamela Hallmark, Pearl Brooking, Delia Commons, Rosemary Harding, Phyllis Harding,
Muriel Johnson, Wilmot Cliff, Dorothy Taylor, Doris Jefferson;
2nd row: Rosemary Nunn, Carolyn Sampson, Janice Davies, Gillian Robinson, Doreen Sharland,
Muriel Clarke, Hilary Field, Violet Quick, Evelyn Hine, Florence Manning, Ruth Hobbs;
front: Harold Joint, Reg Sampson, Betty Sampson, Vera Brimacombe, Henrietta Sandover, William Peek,
Ann Pethybridge.

Loddiswell Fair

Until the 1930s a Fair was held on Whit Mondays, and its main attraction was two sets of swing boats, four to a set. One set was erected near the Congregational Hall and the other was on the Green by the Turks Head Inn. People could have four swings and then the attendant pulled a lever to stop them.

There was a shooting gallery outside Gayfield garages which were then Wilfred Paynter's stables. Firing was at targets which were moved along by turning a handle. Stalls were erected for the sale of sweets and other items. Lunches of bread, cheese and a pint of cider were served at the two public houses.

LODDISWELL WOMEN'S INSTITUTE

Loddiswell W.I. began with a preliminary meeting on 23 November 1920 followed by a meeting on the 17 February 1921 when Miss Collins was elected President. Membership in 1922 reached 47 and peaked to 70 plus in the 1960s to the '80s. It has now declined to less than 30 but the average attendance at meetings is high. Various skills were learned in the early days, from hat making to demonstrations of jam and jelly making. Homecrafts still form the basis for various competitions but other skills are taught, including quilling and the making of dough ornaments.

Over the years the Institute has won several cups at W.I. exhibitions for craft and cooking. In 1987 Loddiswell entered the South Hams Home Economics Exhibition which was held at Malborough Village Hall and 12 members succeeded in winning all six cups in their classes, much to the delight of President Audrey Hine.

Subscriptions were 2 shillings per annum in 1920 and by 1998 they had risen to £14.50. Hire of the hall cost 2s.6d. in 1920 and £6.50 in 1998.

One of the outings in 1939 was a mystery trip to Torcross, returning through Aveton Gifford and the lanes to the President's home at Blackwell Parks for supper. Mrs Conran was the then President. Blackwell Parks was again the venue for supper in 1997 after a walk through Andrew's Wood and the hostess was W.I. Secretary Ann Kelly. The beautiful countryside of the South West has provided many opportunities for tours to places of interest but the Institute has also ventured further afield to Paris and Majorca.

The W.I. has played an important part in the lives of Loddiswell women through the years and is preparing to celebrate its 80th birthday in the year 2000.

Maypole dancing at the Women's Institute Golden Jubilee Fête, 20 June 1970.
(Left to right) standing: Christine Brooking, Beverley Pridham, Sally Clarke (behind), Suzanne Brimacombe, Janet Birmingham, Denise Pridham, Pamela Ryder, Judith Hyne (standing in front); kneeling: Debra Venn, Yvonne Lethbridge, Carole Hyne, Lisa Beckley, Karen Tickner, Debbie Townsend, Rosemary Perring.

Loddiswell W.I., 1999.
(Left to right) back: Margaret Carpenter, Lynn Satterley, Josie Groves, Vi Hine, Jean Wood, Ellen Bardens, Jean Tarr, Joan Allen, Chris Rockey, Hilary Field, Barbara Harrad-Moore, Connie Faulkner, Beryl Brooking, Jean Hallam, Sally Dutton, Muriel Clarke;
front: Ruth Hyne, Sheila Harvey, Jane Taylor, Ann Kelly, Sue Ryder, Hilda Harvey, Susan Freeman, Sylvia Hallam. (Absent: Dee Nash, Marjorie Vooght, Eunice Bidgood).

Loddiswell W.I. at Hazelwood, 1930. (Left to right) back: Mrs Rickard (cook at Hazelwood), Eva Kernick, Laura Yalland, Ethel Whittle, Mrs Martin (Weekmoor), Annie Pedrick, Ethel Hine, Miss Chaffe, Mrs Lee (Wrinkley), Ethel Eastley, Winnie Skinner;
centre: Mrs Collins (Hazelwood), Mrs Bryant, Sheelagh Taylor, Hon. Mrs Joan Peek, Gladys Conran, Betty Wise, Mrs Chaffe, Rosa Preston;
front: Laura Bowden, Beryl Bowden, Marjory Sandover, Nellie Sandover, Nellie Lee, Miss Owen, Alice Taylor, Sheila Taylor.

LODDISWELL VILLAGE HALL

Parish funds have been used three times to secure the Village Hall for public use. In 1872 the Arundell Charity gave a piece of land for the building of the Church School, playground and Schoolmaster's House. The reddish stone used for the building came from Loddiswell Quarry which was just south of Fosse's Wood near the road to Loddiswell Bridge. Subscriptions were invited from friends of the church and parishioners towards the cost of the building. It ceased to be used as a school when the Church School and the British School merged in 1916 and then became the village meeting and function room.

The Church School, later the Village Hall and School House, 1910.

At the beginning of the Second World War pupil numbers increased with evacuees from the towns and more classrooms were needed. The Church School was used again for a class and this continued until 1956 when a timber classroom was added to the British School, by then known as the Primary School. Unfortunately the use of the Church School for education during the war years allowed it to be entangled in the 1944 Education Act whereby any Church School then being used for education automatically became the property of the Diocesan Board of Finance for disposal as they wished. This occurred in 1958

and parishioners were concerned that they would lose their main meeting place.

The Parochial Church Council enquired of the Diocesan Board the price at which they would sell and learned it would be £400. The PCC had no funds for this purpose so the Arundell Charity offered to pay £20 a year for 20 years to secure the Hall. By 1977 only one final payment was due, and enquiries were made of the PCC about its intentions for the future of the premises. A statement was issued by the churchwardens and hall trustees that the revenue received from the use of the hall was insufficient to meet the expenses, and the property would be offered for sale at current market value believed to be about £3000 or it would be leased to a charitable trust representing the organisations of the village.

The Parish Council agreed to pay for the purchase of the property over a period of four years which would be vested in the Loddiswell Playing Fields Charity on condition that they raised between £4500 and £5000 to renovate and modernise the building for public use.

The renamed Loddiswell Playing Fields and Village Hall Trust undertook to extend the hall, taking in the billiard room, and to build and equip a kitchen to modern standards and construct new toilets.

Loddiswell W.I. Fete at the pavilion, 1966.

1. Ruth Hyne 2. Kathleen Brooking 3. Hazel Hine 4. Ethel Eva Hine 5. Muriel Clarke 6. Christine Edgecombe 7. Mary Quick 8. Florence Manning 9. Doris Sharland 10. Mary Watkins 11. Gladys Hodge 12. Maureen Jeffery 13. Nell Scobell 14. Kathy Perring 15. Christian Michell 16. Susan Freeman 17. Gillian Taylor 18. Kathleen Dare 19. Joan King 20. Violet Mabin 21. ? 22. Jean Tarr 23. Susie Pethybridge 24. Iris Wallbutton 25. Rosemary Harding 26. Gladys Brooking 27. Marion Hyne 28. Sheelagh Taylor 29. Muriel Carpenter 30. Evelyn Hine 31. ? 32. Mabel Goss 33. Phyllis Harding 34. Lady Buxton 35. Vera Geatches 36. Mrs Wellington 37. ? 38. Hazel Lethbridge 39. Gladys Conran 40. Miss Jones 41. Anne Butler 42. Pearl Brooking 43. Hilda Harvey 44. Doris Pile 45. Nancy Johns 46. Heather Harding 47. Emma Freeman 48. Judy Fry 49. Rose Luscombe 50. Triffy Perraton.

Albert Francis, a retired London photographer, with his dog, Whisky, carrying home the daily paper, 1970.

DOG TRAINING AT LODDISWELL

The Loddiswell Playing Fields have been used for dog training every Thursday morning since 1996. It is open to dogs of all types and ages and lasts for an hour. Denise Pannell started the training in 1986 and the present instructor is Pete George, a retired police dog handler.

The training methods used are based on praise and reward to which the dogs readily respond. The purpose is to train dogs in obedience to the Kennel Club Good Citizen Certificate standard which means training the owners as well (often the most difficult part!) and encouraging all aspects of responsible dog ownership.

Many dogs are pack animals and the classes give the dogs a chance to socialise. Owners have an opportunity to ask advice and to have dog behaviour explained so they can better understand their pets and correct any faults.

Dog training at the Playing Fields with Pete George, 1999.

Loddiswell Euchre Team champions at the New Bridge Inn, c. late 1970s.
Left to right: Owen Elliott, Wallace Tarr, Paul Wills, Wilfred Saunders, Bill Wills, Kevin Webber,
John Webber, Bill Loram (licensee);
sitting: Tony Jarvis, Dorothy Sanders, Joan Webber, Alice Loram, Fred Marks.

Left to right: Hilary Field, Sylvia Hallam, Eunice Bidgood and Ruth Hyne.
Hilary and Ruth began to learn Honiton lacemaking in 1969 and became Devon lace teachers.

LODDISWELL PLAYING FIELDS

A phrase in current politics is that fairness can only be achieved 'on a level playing field'. This is equally true in sport and Loddiswell is fortunate in having one of the most level in the district.

It was at the end of the Second World War that the idea was muted. Funds were being raised within the parish by the Loddiswell Welcome Home Fund to celebrate the return of men and women from the war. A committee was formed in June 1945 to decide the type of welcome that would be appropriate. Mr. L.R. Sampson said that one should remember that not all would return and most of the funds raised should be used for something that would be permanent.

Between Terrace Hill and Loddiswell Butts were two fields that could be purchased. They were known as 'Amery' and 'Cross Park' and were owned by John Edward Hawke of Newton Abbot. The Hon. Mrs Joan Peek offered that, if the fields were purchased, she would have a hall or pavilion built there in memory of her son, Roger, who was killed in the war. Arthur Grant suggested that W.G. Northcott and Co. would be prepared to give a competitive quotation for the construction of double tennis courts. Concerted efforts were made to raise more funds to purchase the fields at £730, to pay for new gates and for the removal of the dividing hedge bank.

After the war, building materials were very scarce as they were needed to rebuild the war-damaged towns and villages but fund-raising continued. Regular whist drives and annual carnivals were arranged, and a series of plays was staged in the Village Hall. Work began on the tennis courts in 1952 and was completed by March 1953 at a cost of £960. Two years later plans for a pavilion were drawn up and the building was opened in 1955. A children's play area of swings and slides was constructed in 1949 and was improved and extended in 1990 with a new slide and rocker. This area is popular with both young children and parents.

The Playing Field is ideal for football and Loddiswell has raised a succession of strong teams

Pavilion re-building team, 1991. Left to right: John Webber, Rodney Brooking, Reg Sampson, Robert Webber, Kevin Webber, Andy Guard.

through the years. It is a good site for the annual Loddiswell Show that commemorated its 50th Anniversary in 1971 and 75th in 1997 (no show was held in 1984) and many other fêtes and sporting events are held there.

By 1990 the pavilion needed renovation as the external weather board had deteriorated and the cedar shingles on the roof were no longer waterproof. It was decided that a concrete block outer leaf should be built incorporating new double-glazed windows and doors, and a new slated roof. The estimated cost would be about £20 000 which would be difficult to raise but, with voluntary labour, the cost would be about half that amount. During the next year £5450 was obtained from grants and a loan of £5000 from the Parish Council repayable over five years. Many people were generous and the loan was repaid on time.

The work was undertaken by a voluntary team lead by John Webber and his sons Robert and Kevin. Rodney Brooking and Reg Sampson completed the workforce who toiled for four hours a week for 18 months. Andy Guard prepared plans for the addition of a store which was incorporated and Bill Reader regularly provided mid-morning tea and biscuits. This was accompanied by his full report of the Loddiswell football teams' recent performances!!

The re-slated pavilion with blocks ready for the rebuilding of the walls.

Loddiswell School's first football team, 1924. (Left to right), back: Henry (Harry) Sargent, headmaster,
William Luscombe, Harold Webber, Alan Baker, Horace Maynard;
centre: Arthur Hine, Ted Guest, Horace Rudell, Alphonso Hine, Harold Joint;
front: Bert Brown, Ben Freeman, Alfred Goss.

FOOTBALL

Henry (Harry) Clement Sargent, who was headmaster at Loddiswell British School (Primary) from 1922 to 1925, encouraged the boys in competitive sports and from those early days the village has always had an enthusiastic team.

At Easter 1938 Loddiswell played against South Brent at Offields Cross near Churchstow and carried off the Harvey Cup. Their Chairman, Jack Guest, invited the team and supporters back to the New Bridge Inn for the celebrations.

The Second World War interrupted play but by 1948 a team was again competing successfully. The players were Owen Elliott, Claude Hine, Ted Quick, Fred Parsliffe, Ron Meares, Ivan Pope, Ted Guest, Ron Stacey and Dick Menge. In 1973 Loddiswell rejoined the South Devon League in Division 6 and by 1982 had climbed to Division 4. Bill Reader recalls: 'I first watched Loddiswell at the Playing Fields on 31 October 1981. They were then in Division 4 of the South Devon League.'

In 1984 they won the Les Bishop Cup by beating Thurlestone 3-0 at Dartmouth. They were promoted to Division 3 during the 1987/8 season when they also won the Les Bishop Cup again by beating Brixham Town 2-1. The West Devon Area Cup and the Devon Intermediate Cup were further triumphs and involved beating Woodbury Salterton 7-2 at Kingsteignton and Channings Wood 2-1 at Dartmouth. This extract comes from the *Herald Express* on 21 November 1988:

Premier Division Kingsteignton Athletic are out of the Herald Cup after an amazing 13 goal thriller with Division Four pacesetters Loddiswell. The tiny South Hams village won the third round tie 7-6 to keep up their remarkable record of having won every game they have played this season. The shocked Kingsteignton boss, Dave Frankpitt had nothing but praise for the way Lodddiswell outplayed their men and they deserved to win. Loddiswell goal scorers were Andy Guard, Malcolm Elliott, John Hyne. Robert Webber and Kevin Webber.

In the 1989/90 season they won promotion to Division 3 and yet again won the Les Bishop Cup by beating Waldron 2-1 at Teignmouth. In 1990/91 they won the Ronald Cup and promotion to Division 2. The Club was successful in reaching Division 1 in 1993/94. A Reserve team was established in the 1992/93 Season entering the League in Division 7 and the following season promoted to Division 6. Bill Reader was proud to be Chairman of the Club in 1993/94 season when both teams were promoted. He has been succeeded by Rodney Brooking whose untiring efforts as Manager have ensured a thriving club.

Victorious winners of the Harvey Cup and their supporters return to the New Bridge Inn, 1938.
Left to right: Laski Elliott, Eric Ryder, Referee (behind – name unknown), boys Maurice and Ivan Pope, ?,
Gladys Eastley (in window), Alfred Pile (wearing cap), Percy Johns, ? Brimb (player), Bill Luscombe,
D. Duncan, Owen Elliott (player), Joe Luscombe, Tom Squires (behind), Dick Menge (Captain), Ern Jefferies,
Claude Hine (player), Wilfred Taylor and Roger, E. Martin (player), M.O. Sarson (League Secretary),
George Finch, John Wallbutton (child), Iris Wallbutton, ? (behind), Mrs Sarson,
George Brooking (Secretary), Jack Eastley (Committee), Jack Guest (Chairman);
sitting: Bill Stone, Annie Stone, Lionel Ryder, Percy Ryder.

Winners of the Harvey Cup again in 1951.
(Left to right) back: Ray Burner, Danny Clarke, Basil Taylor, Gordon Ryder, Fred Parsliffe, Roger Taylor;
front: Tony Hyne, Jack Hine, Percy Johns, Bernard Steer, Ken Hyne.

Loddiswell Ronald Cup winers v Ashburton, 1990/91.
(Left to right) back: Rodney Brooking (Manager), Gary Mills, Malcolm Elliott, Paul Oldman, Ken Carter, Kevin Webber, Andy Guard, Richard Elliott;
front: Kevin Brooking, Neil Tucker, Nick Crispin, Gary King, Robert Webber, Nigel Rundle, Steve Perrins.

Reserve team formed in May 1992 with sponsor, Derek Brooking.
Back row (left to right): Simon Head, Gary Mills, Alex Esplin, Colin Rogers, Derek Brooking (sponsor), Paul Oldman, Geoff Cater, Richard Elliott, Andrew Westlake, Malcolm Elliott;
front row: Nick Crispin, Andy Guard, Andy Bullen, Richard Jarvis.

Scouts and Guides

Loddiswell Girl Guides, 1930. (Left to right) back: Dulcie Farmer, Hazel Finnimore, Gladys Lethbridge, Miss Owen, Gladys Hodge, Doll Taylor;
2nd row: Christian Hamilton's nanny, Sheelagh Taylor, Janet Stocks, Triffy Guest, Nelly Sandover;
front: Doll Yabsley, Queenie Hine, Doris Pile, Christian Hamilton, Dora Pedrick,
Georgette Brooking.

Loddiswell Scouts, 1935. Scout leaders: Mrs Maliphant, Bernard Maliphant, Mrs Mabel Gerry.
(Left to right) back: Francis Hine, Desmond Hill, Harold Pope, ?, Gordon Taylor,
Charlie Brooking, Arthur Brooking, Owen Ryder;
sitting: Jack Pope, Donald Brooking.

LODDISWELL AND DISTRICT OVER SIXTIES CLUB

The Club was founded on 11 December 1979 by three ladies of the village: Anita Hinton, Hazel Lethbridge and Margaret Rundle. It has subsequently become an active part of village life, meeting some 35-40 times a year for both social and charitable purposes. Since the club's inception, membership has risen from 50 to 90 in 1998.

The aims of the club have been to provide a social service for the elderly of the village, to meet for discussions and to listen to speakers with films and slides, and to enjoy coach outings, luncheons, quizzes and games etc.

Over the years many charities have benefited from the club, and the friendship and kindliness of all members is always available to anyone in times of trouble.

Historically the club has been well served by dedicated Committee members who have given their time generously and freely, some serving for ten years or more – Hazel Lethbridge, Walter Hine, Fred Parsliffe, Muriel Johnson – to name but a few. There are of course many others who have aided the club in diverse ways to make it an integral part of the caring community of Loddiswell.

1999 (left to right) standing: Cyril Brooking, Violet Hine, Jean Wood, Albert Kendall, Peggy Riggall, Roger Lethbridge, Barbara Moore, Sheila Elliott, Hilary Field, Jean Tarr, Douglas Tarr, Sylvia Walke, Leslie Walke, Roy Cole, Janet Beckley, Gordon Beckley, Betty Thorns, Monty Pankhurst Doreen Jarvis, Pat Patey, May Wakeham, Jean Hallam, Gwen Seldon, Peter Carpenter, Audrey Pope, Albert Wakeham, Dennis Sharland, Connie Levy, Connie Faulkner;
centre: Dorothy Brooking, Joyce Lethbridge, Hilda Harvey, May Ryder, Joy Ryder, Eunice Bidgood, Ruth Hyne, Sylvia Hallam, Susan Freeman;
front: Hazel Lethbridge, Susie Pethybridge, Muriel Johnson, Jack Hine, Walter Hine, Eveline Hine, Phyllis Robinson, Doris Sharland, Nellie Eaves.

LODDISWELL TENNIS CLUB

Double tennis courts were constructed in the Playing Fields in 1953 and over the next few years young players were encouraged to join a club for lessons and practice. Membership increased to a peak in 1980 when Loddiswell entered one or two teams in the South Hams Tennis League each year.

The surrounding netting was in need of replacing in 1985 and this was done in stages over the next year or two. The tarmac surface of the courts had also begun to deteriorate but the prohibitive cost of resurfacing has prevented the work being carried out.

The Tennis Club could be enlivened by the enthusiasm of a new generation of young players if funds can be raised for re-surfacing.

SHORT MAT BOWLS CLUB

The Short Mat Bowls Club was formed in Loddiswell in June, 1993. At its conception a mat and two sets of woods were loaned by the South Hams District Council Sports Services for £1 a year. A second mat was hired at £8 weekly from REACH.

The initial Committee consisted of: Frank Carpenter (Chairman), Hazel Lethbridge (Treasurer), Sylvia Walke (Secretary), Bert Taylor (Capt) and Valerie Lugger (Fixtures). Some 29 members joined the Club at an annual subscription of £5. It was decided to purchase their own equipment and an application for a grant was made to the Devon Playing Fields Association. This grant amounted to £200 and a further £250 was given by the South Hams Sports Committee. A village bingo raised £285 enabling the Club to purchase a new mat and a second-hand one was bought from Lee Moor at a cost of £300.

The Club meets twice weekly and their skills have gradually improved permitting them to join the South Hams League in the Second Division. In 1997 they won the League Division Cup and the Knock-out Cup.

The present Committee are: Fred King (Chairman), Ron Welham (Treasurer), Tony Cufflin (Secretary) and Maureen Bartlay (Fixtures Secretary). Committee members are: Barry Geldard, Jean Baker, Roy Slater, Barbara Perrett and Valerie Lugger.

Short Mat Bowls Team, 1999.
(Left to right) back: Pam King, Walter Bennett, Barbara Perrett, Ted Westlake, Rosemary Bennett, Jack Hine, Ken Hyne, Tony Cufflin, John Hornsby, Fred King, Barry Geldard, Roy Slater, Maureen Bartley, David Freeman, Jean Wood, Alan Bell, Ron Welham;
front: Valerie Lugger, Wendy Fieldman, Margaret Carpenter, Frank Carpenter, Muriel Clarke, Joan Webber, Brenda Welham.

TABLE TENNIS CLUB

Although Loddiswell no longer has a table tennis team the South Hams League was originally formed due to the keen interest shown by Gordon Beckley. He had played in the North Devon League for some time and contacted a member of the Kingsbridge Police Force who was also interested in starting a local league.

A meeting was held at the Kingsbridge Police Station on 29 October 1969 and enough support was raised to form three divisions which consisted of 32 teams. At that time the charge for each adult was 5 shillings and juniors 2s.6d. – considerably less than today's charge of £3 and £1 respectively.

In the early years Loddiswell won the cup on several occasions with Terry Hockin, John Barry, Roger Taylor and Gordon Beckley (also a member of the League Committee).

LODDISWELL CLASSIC MOTOR CYCLE CLUB

After the end of the First World War the production of motorcycles escalated. At the 1919 Olympia Show there were more than 200 models on display; it put the ownership of a motorcycle within the reach of the rural working man. A few men in Loddiswell owned bikes, including Bill Yabsley who owned a Brough Superior, known as the 'Rolls-Royce' of motorbikes. The new price of this bike would have been approximately £140, but Bill is unlikely to have bought it new. In the 1920s the prices stabilised; an average 500cc bike costing between £60 and £85. Jack Eastley had an AJS which he always rode wearing his trilby hat, Bert Elliott and Jack Hyne both had Triumphs and Bert Brown had a Raleigh.

In the early 1930s after the depression prices reached rock bottom, a Panther 250cc could be bought new for £30 and many more bikes came into the village. Each owner kept their bikes for many years and took great pride in them, doing their own servicing.

After the Second World War many ex WD machines came on the market at prices of between £40 and £70. Nortons, BSA m20s, Matchless 350s and Royal Enfields. Alf Ryder had an ex-American army Indian, which was later fitted to a sidecar when he was married. Later he bought a Norton Big 4 with a sidecar.

In the 1950s twin-cylinder machines were all the rage and many young men had them. Sadly the British motorcycle industry went into decline in the 1960s and '70s when Japanese imports seemed to take over. Improved living standards meant that small cars were more affordable.

The use of motorcycles became popular in the 1990s for pleasure and there is a lot of interest in the restoration of British motorcycles which have become quite valuable; a 1950s bike that cost £200 new can now fetch up to £3000. Russell Baker recently acquired a 1924 Norton H16, single-cylinder side valve 490cc which he is restoring and this is just one of 13 British bikes in the village which have been restored or are under restoration. The bikes range mainly in the 1950 to the 1980 group. Their owners are: Russell Baker, Roger Eastley, Andy Gallagher, Graham Hodge, Ian Hyne, Bill Penwill, Andy Pettitt, Clive Rowe, Brian Rundle, Douglas Tarr, David Wallis and John Webber. Newer bikes are owned by Derek Hine and Chris Rogers.

Harry Eastley on Bert Elliott's Triumph, Jack Hyne on his own Triumph, Hatch Bridge 1928.

SOUTH WEST BANGER RACING

A few Loddiswellians enjoy the fun of banger racing and sometimes manage to win a prize or two. Peter Sweet is usually in the first three of his class and has carried off many awards. Michael Hine and Alan and Derek Brooking have also been successful competitors. A number of races are held on a grass track near Wrangaton ranging from non-contact races for front and rear wheel drive, to 'Big Bangers' races where the object is to barge one's way through to the leading positions. The crowds are thrilled with the final race which is usually a 'Demolition Derby' in which the last surviving banger on the track wins the race.

AUTOCROSS AND RALLYCROSS

John Sampson has enjoyed competing since 1977 when he was second in the Road Rally Championship in a Mini. In the following year he was first in a TR7. Later a TR8 was developed in the farm workshop which was ideally suited to autocross because of its short wheelbase, giving it enormous traction in sticky conditions. It helped him to win first in class for several years in the BTRDA Autocross Championships and to come in the first three in the RAC National Autocross.

In 1995 John began driving in Rallycross and although he managed to win his class found the TR8 was too short a wheelbase on the firm surfaces of tarmac and gravel so a new design was needed. A Rover 200 was assembled with a TVR Tuscan gearbox and Rover 4.5 V8, rear wheel drive and it is the only one of its kind competing in British motorsport.

It order to achieve maximum points it is sometimes necessary to compete as far away as Pembrey in Wales, Brands Hatch in Kent, Mondello Park, Dublin and Valkenswaard in Holland. In 1998 he was again successful, this time winning the trophy of the BRDA British Rallycross Championship.

John Sampson in his Rover 200 winning the BRDA British Rallycross Championship in 1998 at Croft Circuit, Darlington.

LODDISWELL YOUTH CLUB

Loddiswell Youth Club was formed in the early 1970s by John and Joyce Kirby and Ann and Dick Tucker, to encourage the teenage youth members to participate in competitive activities. Suzanne Prout (née Brimacombe) recalls that John Kirby entered them in the Local Youth Club Competition which took place at Mothecombe Beach. The teams had to dig up plastic pots from the sand which contained tokens. Loddiswell Youth Club collected the highest number and won the prize of a minibus. This enabled them to travel more widely and visit other clubs.

John Ellison became the next leader with Ivy Sweet (née Feetenby) as Assistant. In 1977 she took over leadership helped by Anita Hinton, Pearl Wills and Geoff Collins. The minibus began to cost the club excessively and soon after Mac Carter became leader in 1978 the bus was sold. The proceeds provided funds to purchase disco equipment and canoes. Mac encouraged many outside activities, including camping weekends and canoeing trips at Finlake and on the Avon from Aveton Gifford to Bantham.

During the 1980s the Club won the 'Superstars' Trophy for several years running and were winners at the South Hams Youth Association's Swimming Gala at Totnes swimming pool on several occasions.

In 1990 Mac retired and handed over to Margaret Wootton with help from Christine Rockey until 1996. Julie Reeve was the next leader from 1996 assisted by Kirsty Broda and, in 1998, by George Prout. The club provides a once-weekly social evening for members from the age of nine upwards. In the winter months table tennis, snooker, board games and soft indoor football are played and in the summer months activities move to the Playing Fields.

Jamie and Simon Carter canoeing at Thurlestone, 1984.

Carnival Time

Above: Kingsbridge Fair's 500th anniversary in 1971. 'The Puritans' tableaux by Loddiswell Congregational Chapel. Left to right: Roy Scobell, Michael Hine, Dennis Hine, Emma Freeman, Ethel Hine, Ethel Eva Hine, Nell Scobell, Gladys Hodge, Leonard Scobell.

Above: Teddy Girls Thelma Gill and Connie Taylor, 1948.

Right: 'Gorgeous Gussy' Owen Elliott and racing tipster Jack Hine, 1948.

Below: Hilda Harvey and Anne Butler as sailor and Hawaiian girl, 1956.

'Offbeats' in concert at the Village Hall, 1972.
Front row (left to right): Denise Pridham, Cynthia Tarr, Sally Clarke, Carolyn Sampson, Debbie Woodward,
Hazel Lethbridge, Ann Gill; back row: Gillian Robinson, Sara Field, Ann Lethbridge, Janet Beckley,
Gillian Taylor, Christine Brooking, Maureen Jeffery, Hilda Harvey

Elsa Kelly of Blackwell Parks with her ponies and carriage ready to leave for a wedding.

Outing of the Loddiswell Men's Institute in 1925 in Noyce's solid-tyred charabanc.
Seated (left to right): John Hendy, Mrs Mary Rundle, Jack Eastley, Ethel Eastley, Laura Yalland, Mrs Rudell,
Elsie Burman, Annie Stone, ? (boy in foreground), Mr Rudell, Charlie Miller (driver), Norman Eastley,
Gilbert Garland, Jack Hyne;
standing: Arthur Rundle, Harold Pope, Coulton Freeman, George Brooking,
Harry Eastley, Lizzie Pope, Mildred Rundle, Mary Quick, Constance Rundle, Mrs Pile, Doll Bush,
Arthur Rundle (behind), Claude Luscombe, Ida Hine, Ernest Hine.

Day out at Bantham in the 1920s.
Left to right: Louise Hambley, Sarah Guest, Granny Hyne, Nurse Guest, Marion Hyne, Laura Yalland,
Lettie Eastley, Mrs Eastley and daughter Gladys Eastley (with child), Mary Hine.

Seaside outing in the 1930s.
Back row (left to right): Doris Pile, Winnie Seldon, Marjorie Brooking, Muriel Ryder;
front row: Alice Taylor, Rosie Hine, Phyllis Elliott, Cora Ryder.

Seaside outing in the 1930s.
Back row (left to right): Joan Elliott, Evelyn Pile, Eveline Harding, Muriel Stoyles;
front row: Winnie Seldon, Marjorie Brooking, Dolly Ryder, Doris Elliott.

Granny Hyne and the Rev. Maliphant at the pump in Fore Street.

⚔ Anecdotes of Loddiswell Personalities ⚔

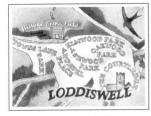

When the New Mill Bridge was being built at the end of the 19th century Loddiswell masons and labourers were employed on the task. William Elliott, the baker, remembered before any bridge building could be done a massive arched timber framework was erected on which to build the stone arches. The timber arches were nearly completed when one of the men fell and as he tumbled grabbed hold of the timberwork. He found he was suspended over the river. Albert Elliott, a mason, reached down to pull him up but found he could not lift him, nor could the poor man help himself. There was only one way out – he released his grip and splashed down into the river. The volume of water saved his fall and he dragged himself to the bank, saturated but unharmed.

During the war years when they finished their Home Guard duties the Cole brothers of Wood Barton would call at the New Bridge Inn for a social drink. One evening after a lengthy session Lionel Ryder called in after a trip to the river with a large salmon. After some negotiating Reg Cole bought it for 2s.6d. pence. As the evening wore on and the effects of the beer became more apparent the salmon was slipped from under Reg's chair, Lionel returned after a little while with it and asked Reg Cole if he would like another salmon – to which he readily agreed paying another 2s.6d.!

POACHING to many locals was a challenge who tried to outwit the WATER BAILIFF and take SALMON under cover of darkness

Drawings by Mike Glanville.

Tom Rundle was the licensee of the Turks Head for many years – even when he retired as publican felt it was a second home and when passing would make a social call. One day after returning from taking his cows from his farm in Town's Lane through the village to their pastures he called in and found the landlady, Mrs Pavey in great distress. Not only was she distressed at loosing her favourite cat but did not know how to dispose of it. Tom consoled her by kindly offering to take the dead cat and put it in his sack. After leaving the Turks Head he wended his way home past the New Bridge Inn where he saw Squire Eastley sitting in the window. On entering the pub Squire asked what Tom was carrying in his bag. Tom replied he had just caught a beautiful rabbit. Owing to the severe war-time shortage of meat Squire Eastley became very interested and offered to buy the rabbit for 2s. (a lot of money in the early 1940s). Tom immediately said 'right and you can have the bag as well' – and Squire Eastley's reaction to the trick has not been disclosed.

Capt W.G. Peek (seated) retires as Chairman of the Parish Council in 1995.
Councillors (left to right): Ted Westlake (Clerk), Derek Brooking, Cyril Freeman, Peter Lethbridge, Reg Sampson, Sue Sweeney, Russell Baker, Hazel Lethbridge.

173

SUBSCRIBERS

Austin J. Adams, West Alvington, Kingsbridge, Devon
Aveton Gifford Project Group, Aveton Gifford, Kingsbridge, Devon
Russell & Jean Baker, Loddiswell, Devon
James R. T. Baker, Gloucester
Nellie R. Baker, Loddiswell, Devon
Francis W. A. Baker, Loddiswell, Devon
Freda Baldwin, Auckland, New Zealand
Arnold & Joan Banham, Loddiswell, Devon
Cliff Beasant & Michele Munro, Loddiswell, Devon
Gordon & Janet Beckley, Loddiswell, Devon
Miss June Bennett, London SW6
Miriam Blakemore, Loddiswell, Devon
Mrs Sheila Bolam (née Hall), Loddiswell Station, Kingsbridge, Devon
Richard & Blodwen Bowen, Loddiswell, Devon
Cynthia M. Branson
Linda & Rafi Brasher, Loddiswell, Devon
Mrs D. Bridger, Loddiswell, Devon
Mrs A. M. Brimacombe, Loddiswell, Devon
Elizabeth J. Broad, Loddiswell, Devon
Rodney J. Brooking, Loddiswell, Devon
Derek A. Brooking, Loddiswell, Devon
Kathleen F. Brooking, Loddiswell, Devon
Myrtle P. Brooking, Loddiswell, Devon
Cyril & Dorothy Brooking, Loddiswell, Devon
Beryl R. Brooking (née Bowden), Loddiswell, Devon
Derek R. Brown, Taplow, Maidenhead, Berks.
Owen Burner, Salcombe, Devon
K. J. Burrow, Bucks Cross, Bideford, Devon
Mr & Mrs John Burt, Loddiswell, Devon
John C. Came, Loddiswell, Devon
Mr & Mrs H. F. J. Camp, Grays, Essex (formerly of Loddiswell, Devon)
Mr Horace Fredrick Camp (formerly of Loddiswell, Devon)
Canon Bob Campbell-Smith, Rector Modbury Team Ministry, Devon
Philip Carpenter, Marlow, Bucks.
Muriel Carpenter, Loddiswell, Devon
Frank & Margaret Carpenter, Loddiswell, Devon
Pauline & Malcolm Carter, Loddiswell, Devon
The Cater family, Loddiswell, Devon
Muriel & Simon Clarke, Loddiswell, Devon
Roy H. Cole, Loddiswell, Devon
John, Alison & Ashley Commons, Loddiswell, Devon
Rev. P. G. H. Cooke, Torquay, Devon
James Corbet, ex Stile Cottage, Loddiswell, Devon
Derek W. Cotter & Mrs Christine Tyers, Loddiswell, Devon
Phyllis C. Court (née Baker), Kingsbridge, Devon
John & June Cowper, Brooking, Totnes, Devon
Mrs Natalie Cropper, Goring-By-Sea, Sussex

Anthony & Maurice Cufflin, Loddiswell, Devon
Rosemary Damerell (née Harding), Scottish Borders
Madalene Daniel, South Australia
Mrs S. Daniels, Plympton, Plymouth, Devon
Alison Davies (née Elliott), Ashford
Francis & Vivien de Beer, Avon Mill, Loddiswell, Devon
Bob, Jill & Jessica Deere, Sydney, Australia
Sara J. Dineen, Teddington, Middlesex
Sally & Stephen Dutton, Loddiswell, Devon
Mrs A. M. Edgcombe, Loddiswell, Devon
Mrs Jacqueline Edwards, Newton Abbot, Devon
Margery Edwards (née Tarr), Loddiswell, Devon
Mr I. R. Elliott, Woodbury Salterton, Exeter, Devon
Laskey J. Elliott, Loddiswell, Devon
Garry, Karen, Sophie & Amy Elliott, Loddiswell, Devon
J. S. & D. M. Elliott, Little Chillaton Farm, Loddiswell, Devon
Owen & Sheila Elliott, Loddiswell, Devon
W. J. Ellis, 1 Town Park, Loddiswell, Devon
Kelvin & Jan Ellis, Loddiswell Station, Kingsbridge, Devon
Olive E. Ellis, Loddiswell, Devon
Barbara Elson, Aveton Gifford, Kingsbridge, Devon
Sally & Phillip Errett, Loddiswell, Devon
C. R. & S. L. Evans, Loddiswell, Devon
Roger H. Evans, Salcombe, Devon
Elizabeth A. Evans (née Andrews), Brixton, Plymouth, Devon
Richard & Lin Fairfax, Loddiswell, Devon
Patrick J. Field, Loddiswell, Devon
Margaret Foulkes, Rattery, Devon
Malcolm & Diana Frame, Loddiswell, Devon
S. Yvonne Franklin (née Parsliffe), Evesham, Worcs.
Nick & Trish Freeman, Kingsbridge, Devon
Catherine Freeman, Canada
Cyril & Angela Freeman, Loddiswell, Devon
Malcolm G. Freeman, Three Leg Cross, Ticehurst, Sussex
Steve & Angie Freeman, Totnes, Devon
Susan Freeman (née Wallbutton), Loddiswell, Devon
Valerie Garland, Loddiswell, Devon
Barry Geldard & Maureen Bartley, Kingsbridge, Devon
Frances & Phil George, Loddiswell, Devon
Edward George, Loddiswell, Devon
Louise George, Loddiswell, Devon
Rachel George, Loddiswell, Devon
Mrs R. A. Gill, London SW19
Thelma E. Gill, Loddiswell, Devon
Joanna Gillard, Totnes, Devon
Michael W. Goss, York
Donald & Rita Greig, Woodleigh, Kingsbridge, Devon
Mrs Barbara Groves, Penryn, Cornwall
Peter Gunter, Farthings, Bantham

Denis Hainsworth, Woodleigh, Kingsbridge, Devon
Sylvia Hallam, Loddiswell, Devon
Mr S. R. Hallett, Totnes, Devon
Monica Hann, Redruth, Cornwall
Mr M. R. Hannah, St Cleer, Liskeard, Cornwall
Gay Harding (née Ridd), Ex Wrinkley Farm, Loddiswell, Devon
Dr S. J. Hargreaves, Loddiswell, Devon
Colin & Sandra Harvey, Plymstock, Devon
Hilda M. Harvey & Nigel, Loddiswell, Devon
Trevor Harvey & Veronica, Gloucester
Stephen J. Herriman, Blackwell Park, Loddiswell, Devon
Gerald P. Hill, Loddiswell, Devon
Michael H. Hine, Loddiswell, Devon
Roger Hine, Tavistock, Devon
Walter Hine, Loddiswell, Devon
Jack & Rose Hine, Loddiswell, Devon
Paul Hine, Launceston, Cornwall
Mr Timothy W. Hine, Loddiswell, Devon
Dennis James Hine, Loddiswell, Devon
D. Hine, Loddiswell, Devon
Michael E. Hine, Dry Doddington, Lincs
Hugh Derrick Hiscock, Dryden, Ontario, Canada
Carol Hodder, Aveton Gifford, Devon
John & Mary Hodder, Aveton Gifford, Devon
Graham J. Hodge, Loddiswell, Devon
Dr Rod Holcombe, Kingsbridge, Devon
Jamie & Pearl Holford
Geoffrey Holt M.R.C.V.S., Chevithorne, Loddiswell, Devon
Mr Peter Homburger, Colorado, U.S.A.
Peter Homburger, Colorado, U.S.A.
Denise Hopwood (née Brooking), Loddiswell, Devon
John Hornsby (Postmaster), Loddiswell, Devon
Patrick J. T. Horton, Halesowen, West Midlands
John W. T. Horton, Weston-Super-Mare
Mrs L. Hosking, Loddiswell, Devon
John Hosking, Hatch, Loddiswell, Devon
Irene Hulse, Loddiswell, Devon
Michael Hyne, Loddiswell, Devon
Richard & Debbie Hyne, Hemel Hempstead, Herts.
Stuart & Salwa Hyne, Loddiswell, Devon
Kenneth & Ruth Hyne, Loddiswell, Devon
James & Veronica Hyne, Carlyon Bay, Cornwall
Victor & Lyn Ibbetson, Loddiswell, Devon
Janet & James C. Ivey, Truro, Cornwall
Keith & Clarice James, Barnstaple, Devon
Peter & Maureen H. Jeffery, Loddiswell, Devon
S. P. Jeffery, Tavistock, Devon
Mrs W. Jeffery, Loddiswell, Devon
J. & V. Jeffery, Crewkerne, Somerset
Mrs Valerie Johnson, Follaton, Totnes, Devon
Alan Jones, Hope Cove, Kingsbridge, Devon
Elsa J. Kelly, Blackwell Park, Loddiswell, Devon
Bernard & Anne Kelly, Blackwell Park, Loddiswell, Devon

Gregory Kemsley, Kingsbridge, Devon

Joanna Kendall Acourt, Loddiswell, Devon

Sunnette Kennard, Auckland, New Zealand

W. K. Kernick, Loddiswell, Devon

Ivor & Joan King, Loddiswell, Devon

Mr Douglas Knight, South Pool, Kingsbridge, Devon

The Knights, Church Cottage, Woodleigh, Kingsbridge, Devon

Mr Brian Knox, Loddiswell, Devon

Arthur Edwin & Hazel Ann Lethbridge, Loddiswell, Devon

Joyce Lethbridge, Loddiswell, Devon

Robert & Sally Lewis (née Clarke), Ivybridge, Devon

Ann Lidstone (née Rogers), Kingsbridge, Devon

Mr & Mrs R. T. Ling, Loddiswell, Devon

Loddiswell Primary School, Loddiswell, Devon

Ian & Hayley Lowcock, Sunflower Cottage, Loddiswell, Devon

Mrs A. Luscombe, Ipplepen, Newton Abbot, Devon

Mr & Mrs Richard Luttman & family, Loddiswell, Devon

Eric Mabin, Florida, U.S.A.

John & Hazel Mabin, Fremington, Devon

Bernard Maliphant, Merthyr Tydfil, Mid Glamorgan

Dr Rodney Maliphant, Exeter, Devon

Dr Gordon Maliphant, Wellington, Somerset

John & Margaret Mann, Kingskerswell, Devon

John D. Marsh, Loddiswell, Devon

Mr C. E. Marshall, Loddiswell, Devon

David A. E. Martin, Loddiswell, Devon

Christine Martin (née Withers), Broadclyst, Nr Exeter, Devon

Alex & Cynthia Marwood, Kingsbridge, Devon

Lorna Masters (née Ridd), Ex Wrinkley Farm, Loddiswell, Devon

Ray & June Mathieson, New Zealand

Mr J. H. Mallen & Mrs D. J. Matthews, Newbridge House, Loddiswell, Devon

Dr Rosemary Mattingly (née Willing), Exeter, Devon

B. J. Maxwell, Loddiswell, Devon

Sarah & Peter McAughley, Loddiswell, Devon

Mrs Diana Mead, Woolston, Loddiswell, Devon

Christopher B. Meathrel, Westbourne, Bournemouth, Dorset

Janet Meehan, Highgate, London NW5

Jodie & Alan Milton, Loddiswell, Devon

Elizabeth C. Montague, Loddiswell, Devon

Malcolm G. Montague, Loddiswell, Devon

Martin & Felicity Nash (née Harvey), Rustington, West Sussex

Francis & Marion Newman, Strete, Dartmouth, Devon

Mrs Pauline A. Nicholson (née Ryder), Ivybridge, Devon

Mrs H. Northmore, Holbeton, Plymouth, Devon

Alec & Sylvia Nunn, Loddiswell, Devon

Michael & Carolyn O'Brien, Cobham, Surrey

Mr M. Pankhurst, Loddiswell, Devon

David & Joan Parkes, ex Woolston House, Loddiswell, Devon

Patrick J. Parsliffe, Kingsbridge, Devon

Dolly M. Parsliffe, Loddiswell, Devon

Joan Parsons, Rattery, Devon

Emma E. Pascoe, U.S.A.

Russell W. Pascoe, London

Anne E. Pascoe, Loddiswell, Devon

Michael B. Passman, Loddiswell, Devon

Zoe Patey, Harlow, Essex

Sir William Peek, Loddiswell, Devon

A. Mary Perring, Kingsbridge, Devon

Donald E. Pethybridge, Reads Farm, Loddiswell, Devon

Mary & John Pettitt, Loddiswell, Devon

Daniel Pettitt, Loddiswell, Devon

Ravi, Joanne, Conor & Kira Pillai, Greenford, Middlesex

Ivan & Audrey Pope, Loddiswell, Devon

Brian Pope, Loddiswell, Devon

Mrs D. Powlesland, St Budeux, Plymouth, Devon

John & Pat Pritchett, Loddiswell, Devon

Simon, Janet, Helena, Alison & Mark Procter, Fisherbeck, Loddiswell, Devon

George Prout & family, Loddiswell, Devon

Reeta Mary Pryce (née Hine), Loddiswell, Devon

Andrew & Kathleen Punchard, Woolston and Stanton, Devon

June M. Puttick, Eastbourne, Sussex

Mrs Linda Quick, Wembury, Plymouth, Devon

Mr E. F. Quick, Saltash, Cornwall

Margaret Read (née Hine), Cambridgeshire

Mr William & Mrs Juanita M. Reader, Loddiswell, Devon

Mrs E. R. Reeve, Woodleigh, Kingsbridge, Devon

Arthur F. & Peggy Riggall, Loddiswell, Devon

Nicholas Francis Rockey, Loddiswell, Devon

Helen Anne Rockey, Loddiswell, Devon

Cecil & Sybil Rogers, Malborough, Kingsbridge, Devon

Bob & Margaret Rogers, Oxford

Chris & Jane Rogers, Loddiswell, Devon

Jane Rose, Loddiswell, Devon

J. Rundle, Loddiswell, Devon

O. W. J. Rundle, Harrow, Middlesex

Mrs E. M. Ryder, West Alvington, Devon

Sue Ryder, Loddiswell, Devon

John & Rosemary Sampson, Woolston Farm, Loddiswell, Devon

Reg & Betty Sampson, Loddiswell, Devon

Andrew W. Sampson, Loddiswell, Devon

Rev. Donald J. Sampson, Sutton Coldfield, West Midlands

Leslie W. Sampson, Oswestry, Shropshire

Lynn & Ian Satterley & Mrs Violet Hine, Loddiswell, Devon

Alan Saville, Hatch Arundell, Loddiswell, Devon

Alistair & Eileen Scott, Ashburton, Devon

Christine Scott (née Rogers), Idestone, Devon

Mr Martyn Seldon, Gloucester

Mrs Gwen P. Seldon, Loddiswell, Devon

Julian Seldon, Saltash, Cornwall

Eric Shaw, Stoke On Trent, Staffs.

Anthony P. Shute, Plymouth, Devon

C. M. & K. E. Shute, Woodleigh, Devon

Christine A. Simpson (née Brooking), Modbury, Devon

Mrs P. Skinner, Loddiswell, Devon

Mr & Mrs J. P. Slade, Loddiswell, Devon

Mr A. E. & Mrs S. M. Slaughter, Loddiswell, Devon

Bob & Sylvia Smith, Canada

J. Smith, Woodleigh, Kingsbridge, Devon

Mrs V. A. Spooner, Loddiswell, Devon

Brian & Linda Staplehurst, Plymouth, Devon

Colin & Vicky Staplehurst, Malborough, Devon

Georgina Stevens, Hornsey, London

William F. Stone, (orig. Ledstone/ Goveton)

Keith, Christine & Penny-Anne Stott, Loddiswell, Devon

Barry D. Sweeney, Loddiswell, Devon

Irene Sweeney

Mrs Jean & Mr Douglas G. Tarr, Loddiswell, Devon

W. Tarr, Loddiswell, Devon

Bert & Jane Taylor, Higher Greystones Farm, Loddiswell, Devon

Basil J. Taylor, Loddiswell, Devon

Beverly Teague, Crackington Haven, Cornwall

Martyn & Stephanie Thompson

Wendy L. Thomson, Cookham, Berks.

R. J. L. Thomson, Gt. Missenden

Mrs Julia Tickner, Loddiswell, Devon

Torquay Central Library, Torquay, Devon

Rev. N. A. F. Townend, North Petherton, Bridgwater, Somerset

Mrs Joan Tyler, Exeter, Devon

Mrs Barbara Vermeulen, Exeter, Devon

Gladys M. Vincent, Sidbury, Devon

B. M. Wakeham, Loddiswell, Devon

Mrs F. Wakeham, Loddiswell, Devon

D. H. Walke, Eastcote, Ruislip, Middlesex

Sylvia & Leslie Walke, Loddiswell, Devon

John F. W. Walling, Newton Abbot, Devon

Mrs Delia Wallis, Loddiswell, Devon

Mr R. I. & Mrs F. Watkins, Wem, Shropshire

John & Joan Webber, Loddiswell, Devon

Kevin J. Webber, Loddiswell, Devon

Larry Welch, Port Angeles, U.S.A.

Ted & Mary Westlake, Loddiswell, Devon

Brother Wilfred, The Priory, Lamacraft Farm, Start Point, Devon

Richard L. Willing, Victoria, Australia

Richard & Celia Willing, South Australia

Percival Harry Withers, Woodleigh, Nr Kingsbridge, Devon

Eleanor Withnell, Loddiswell, Devon

Edmund Withnell, Loddiswell, Devon

Rev. & Mrs R. Withnell, Loddiswell, Devon

Juliet Withnell, Loddiswell, Devon

Mrs Jean Wood, Loddiswell, Devon

Miss Rachael Woollam, Loddiswell, Devon

Also available in the Community History Series:

Further information:

If you would like to order a book or find out more about having your parish featured in this series, please contact The Editor, Community History Series, Halsgrove House, Lower Moor Way, Tiverton Business Park, Tiverton, Devon, EX16 6SS, tel: 01884 243242 or visit us at http://www.halsgrove.com If you are interested in a particular photograph in this volume, it may be possible to supply you with a copy of the image.

*Albert Kendall on his 1927 B.S.A.
round-tank, two-gear motorbike at
Coombe Farm.*